C0-AZM-579

MONEY SMARTS

→ THE GUIDE TO →

TAX-SAVING

INVESTING

HOW TO B•U•I•L•D YOUR WEALTH
BY MASTERING THE BASIC STRATEGIES

ALSO BY DAVID L. SCOTT

The Guide to Personal Budgeting (Money Smarts)
The Guide to Investing in Bonds (Money Smarts)
The Guide to Investing in Common Stocks (Money Smarts)
The Guide to Investing in Mutual Funds (Money Smarts)
The Guide to Buying Insurance (Money Smarts)
The Guide to Managing Credit (Money Smarts)
Understanding and Managing Investment Risk and Return
Dictionary of Accounting
How Wall Street Works
Fundamentals of the Time Value of Money
The Investor's Guide to Discount Brokers
Stretching Your Income:
101 Ways to Help You Cope with Inflation
Security Investments
Finance
Wall Street Words

MONEY SMARTS

THE GUIDE TO
TAX-SAVING
INVESTING

HOW TO B•U•I•L•D YOUR WEALTH
BY MASTERING THE BASIC STRATEGIES

by David L. Scott

The Globe Pequot Press

OLD SAYBROOK, CONNECTICUT

Copyright © 1995 by David L. Scott

All rights reserved. No part of this book may be reproduced or trans-
mitted in any form by any means, electronic or mechanical, including
photocopying and recording, or by any information storage or re-
trieval system, except as may be expressly permitted by the 1976
Copyright Act or by the publisher. Requests for permission should be
made in writing to The Globe Pequot Press, P.O. Box 833, Old Saybrook, Connecticut 06475.

Library of Congress Cataloging-in-Publication Data

Scott, David Logan, 1942–
    The guide to tax-saving investing : how to build your wealth by
mastering the basic strategies / David L. Scott. — 1st ed.
        p.   cm.   —   (Money smarts)
    Includes index.
    ISBN 1-56440-395-5
    1. Investments—United States. 2. Investments—Taxation—United
States. 3. Tax shelters—United States. I. Title. II. Series: Scott,
David Logan, 1942–   Money smarts
HG4910.S3918   1994
332.6—dc20   94-31605
                                                              CIP

Manufactured in the United States of America
First Edition/First Printing

Contents

This book's purpose is to provide accurate and authoritative information on the topics covered. It is sold with the understanding that neither the author nor the publisher is rendering legal, financial, accounting, or other professional services. Neither the Globe Pequot Press nor the author assumes any liability resulting from action taken based on the information included herein. Mention of a company name does not constitute endorsement.

Introduction

Someone, perhaps you, should write a song titled "Tax Saving on My Mind" that could then become our country's new national anthem. Everyone wants to pay less taxes, regardless of the benefits the person receives from the government. By March and early April, nearly every person who files a tax return begins wondering what could have been done to reduce his or her income tax liability. Some individuals, mainly people with large incomes and big tax bills, are searching for tax-saving ideas during the entire year.

The Guide to Tax-Saving Investing addresses how you can save taxes through the investments you make. If you currently place all your savings in certificates of deposit that pay interest income that is fully taxable, you may be able to utilize the ideas presented in this book to save substantial amounts of taxes. You don't have to be a millionaire investing many thousands of dollars in order to benefit from reading the pages of this book. Many of the investments that are discussed can be readily purchased by individuals and families with only modest amounts of money to invest.

Keep in mind that you should generally be in at least the 28 percent tax bracket in order to benefit from tax-advantaged investments. These investments produce even more tax savings if you pay federal taxes on your highest income at rates of 31, 36, or 39.6 percent. Even larger tax savings are possible if you reside in a state and/or city that imposes an income tax. If you are currently paying federal taxes at a rate of 15 percent, you can probably benefit more from choosing regular investments that often offer higher pretax yields.

Never select an investment solely on promised tax savings to the exclusion of economic fundamentals and common sense. Investments are valuable because of the current income and/or increases in value they provide. Being able to defer or shelter income from taxation is an added benefit. You should always avoid investments or investment transactions that you find too complicated to understand. Many intelligent individuals have been sold a pig in a poke because they were too eager to cut the government out of their investment income. Stick to proven investments you understand, and let the pros spend their time and money on exotic investments with great promises of tax savings.

Although the material in this book is believed to be accurate at the time of publication, you must be aware that tax laws change. Thus, it is very important that you check on current tax laws when you begin the process of selecting an investment to purchase.

David L. Scott
Valdosta, Georgia

CHAPTER 1

All You Ever Wanted to Know about Taxes, and More

Taxes, the main source of federal, state, and local government revenues, pay for highways, buildings, public education, airplanes, stop signs, rockets, and the salaries of millions of public employees. Governments borrow when tax revenues are insufficient to meet their spending needs. Governments raise a large amount of tax revenues from levies on personal incomes, including most or all of your investment income. Your personal income tax liability is a function of your gross income adjusted for certain deductions and exemptions. Gains and losses from the sale of investment assets affect the amount of taxes you will be required to pay. The federal income tax is structured to tax different levels of income at different rates. Currently, federal tax rates range from 15 percent to nearly 40 percent.

Taxes are an important aspect of nearly every adult's life. Your paycheck is adjusted for taxes, just as contributions you make to charitable organizations are probably influenced by the taxes you expect to save. Taxes affect the cost of owning a home, and tax considerations probably influence the votes you cast in local, state, and national elections. Taxation of investment income is also an important consideration when you are deciding on investments to purchase, especially if you earn a substantial income that is taxed at a relatively high rate.

Why Taxes?

A world devoid of governments would be a world without taxes. This may sound like utopia, but don't hold your breath, because it isn't a forecast. Taxation represents one of several methods by which governments raise money to pay for the goods and services they are called on to provide. Governments lack the major sources of revenue available to other sectors of the economy and must rely on taxes to finance the majority of their expenditures. Unlike businesses, governments produce few goods and services that can be sold, especially at a profit. Likewise, governments don't have wage and investment income that is earned by individuals and families. Without these sources of income, governments have little choice but to finance their spending needs by assessing individuals and businesses.

Governments continually search for additional funds to pay for the seemingly endless needs of their citizens, businesses, and bureaucrats. At the local level taxes support spending for libraries, schools, stadiums, roads, buildings, fire and police protection, and the salaries of county and municipal employees. States levy taxes to pay for highway construction, public colleges, buildings and equipment, law enforcement, and the acquisition and upkeep of recreation areas. The federal government levies taxes in order to be able to provide its citizens with an interstate highway system, health services, a capable military force, an effective Internal Revenue Service, thousands of parks and monuments, and a zillion other things.

Taxes as One of Several Sources to Finance Government Spending

Taxation is not the only means for financing government spending. Governments at all levels regularly borrow funds that augment their tax revenues. In the 1980s and early 1990s, the federal government *annually* borrowed hundreds of billions of dollars to cover expenditures that exceeded the hundreds of billions of dollars of tax revenues it collected. Governments at all levels also levy a variety of user fees to pay for parks, bridges, transit systems, parking complexes, and sports stadiums, where users rather than taxpayers are expected to bear the cost of the projects. These fees, however, are frequently supplemented by special taxes.

In general, governments borrow because public officials

> Make it a point to determine your marginal income tax rate at the federal, state, and local levels. These are the rates you should use when you calculate an investment's after-tax return. If someone else does your taxes, ask the preparer about your tax bracket.

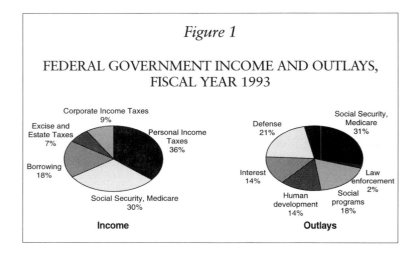

Figure 1

FEDERAL GOVERNMENT INCOME AND OUTLAYS, FISCAL YEAR 1993

are unable or unwilling to collect the full amount of taxes that would be necessary to cover spending. Suppose New Mexico State officials plan to spend $1.2 billion during a period when the state is expected to raise only $1 billion in taxes. Unless New Mexico has previously accumulated a surplus on which it can draw (i.e., in previous years the state was able to generate more in tax revenues than it spent, thus accumulating a surplus), $200 million of borrowing will be required to finance the $200 million deficit created by the excess of spending over income. Of course, state officials could revise the budget and reduce spending to $1 billion, the projected level of tax revenues. A considerable decrease in spending would allow the state to avoid the need to borrow. Reducing spending and/or raising taxes is not always easy to accomplish, especially during or just prior to an election year.

Choosing to fund government spending with current tax

revenues requires that taxpayers pay for goods and services during the period the goods and services are delivered. In other words, government officials are restricted to spending only the amount provided by tax collections. This type of financing, sometimes referred to as *pay-as-you-go spending*, is the same as when individuals choose to pay cash and avoid credit purchases.

In contrast to pay-as-you-go, a government that purchases goods and services with borrowed money operates on the philosophy of *buy now, pay later*. Borrowing pushes payments into the future and allows people to enjoy current consumption while they postpone until later, perhaps much later, the pain of paying for the goods and services they consume. Long-term borrowing and continual refinancing of debts (i.e., borrowing to pay off the balance on a previous loan) can push payments so far into the future that subsequent generations end up being taxed to pay for goods and services enjoyed by their parents and grandparents.

Taxes vs. Borrowing

Neither taxes nor borrowing is without drawbacks. Taxes nearly always anger the individuals and businesses that are required to part with their money. Citizens of all stripes often have the attitude that the only fair tax is paid by

> You may be disappointed by an investment that is purchased primarily for tax reasons. The returns may turn out to be less than you expected at the time you purchased the investment. You may also find that tax law changes result in fewer tax benefits than you expected.

someone else. Thus, a higher tax rate on personal incomes above $140,000 is not a great concern for taxpayers, who, because they earn less than this amount, will not be affected. Critics and skeptics question whether they can expect to get their money's worth from a system in which governments squander tax revenues at the same time that many of their fellow citizens avoid paying their fair share of taxes. People dislike taxes to such an extent that they typically vote against politicians who propose or support new taxes, regardless of how desperately additional revenues are needed.

Borrowing is the alternative with the least amount of immediate pain because payment is postponed to another day, year, or decade. Government use of debt to pay for the goods and services it supplies is analogous to individual use of credit cards or bank loans to pay for purchases of home furnishings, appliances, and automobile repairs. Both government and individual borrowing allow the enjoyment of goods and services while postponing pain of payment until later. A strong antitax public sentiment combined with demands for increased levels of government goods and services has caused governments at all levels to regularly rely on borrowed funds.

The major disadvantage to government borrowing is the accompanying interest charges that increase the eventual cost of goods and services provided to taxpayers. Borrowing also facilitates spending that would ordinarily be postponed or not take place at all. Increased costs associated with interest charges on borrowed money cause current and future taxpayers to eventually be burdened with higher taxes, fewer goods and services, or even more borrowing. Suppose the state of Montana borrows $30 million for ten years at 6

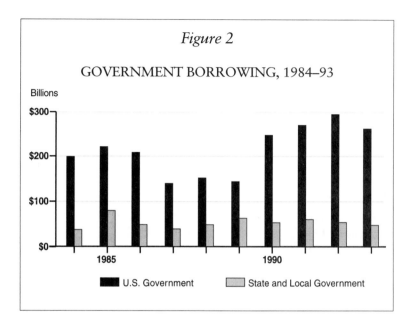

Figure 2

GOVERNMENT BORROWING, 1984–93

Billions

percent annual interest to pay for the acquisition and development of a state recreation area. There isn't anything necessarily unwise or unethical about borrowing to support this project, because the recreation area will provide many years of enjoyment for the state's residents. The decision to borrow, however, means that the state's taxpayers will be required to cough up an extra $18 million for interest charges (6 percent of $30 million for ten years) that must be paid to the lender *in addition to* repaying the $30 million that is borrowed. The total repayment of $48 million when debt financing is used compares to a total cost of only $30 million if Montana officials choose to pay for the recreational area with current tax revenues.

Fundamentals of Income Taxes

Governments utilize an assortment of taxes and fees to finance their expenditures. Local governments rely primarily on property taxes and sales taxes, while most state governments choose to tax both consumption (e.g., a sales tax) and individual and business income. Despite recent tax increases by state and local governments to pay for educational needs, prisons, roads, and a host of programs mandated by the federal government, the individual income tax levied by the federal government has the greatest impact on most individual investors. While states may tax individual and family income at a rate of 4 to 6 percent (some are higher, others lower, and a few have no income tax at all), the federal tax on income begins at 15 percent and tops out at nearly 40 percent, a rate that is considerably higher than the highest rate levied by any state or municipality. Because income taxes, especially those levied by the federal government, affect investors more than any other assessment, this chapter will be largely devoted to a discussion of the federal income tax.

Step One: Calculate Gross Income

Not all the money you receive during a year is taxable. Gifts of money and property you receive from your parents, grandparents, aunt, or anyone else are not taxable as income to you and, unless the gifts have substantial value, are not taxable to the donor. Proceeds received from life insurance are not taxable to you as income, and an insurance settlement on a stolen car or weather-related damage to your home is not taxable. Property you receive from the distribution of a deceased relative's estate is not taxable as income,

---

Figure 3

AN OUTLINE FOR CALCULATING YOUR FEDERAL INCOME TAX

Wages
+ Interest and dividend income
+ Net capital gains
+ Other income
———————
= Gross income

– Adjustments to income
———————
= Adjusted gross income

– Standard deduction or itemized deductions
– Exemptions
———————
= Taxable income

× Tax rate(s)
———————
= Tax on taxable income

– Tax credits
———————
= Tax liability

---

although it may be subject to a state inheritance tax. Federal tax law also permits certain *exclusions* for purposes of calculating your income tax liability. For example, U.S. citizens living and working in a foreign country are permitted to exclude a certain amount of their earned income when they calculate their income tax liability to the United States.

Certain investments produce cash that is not taxed. Interest income from most bonds issued by states and municipal-

ities is not taxable, and money received from selling investment assets such as stocks and bonds is not taxable unless a
profit is earned. If you purchase one hundred shares of
Coca-Cola common stock for $4,500 and later sell the
shares for the same price, no tax is due. Certain investments
produce income that would generally be taxable except for
the fact that certain expenses related to the assets are allowed as offsets against income. Real estate investments
often provide substantial deductible expenses. Deductible
expenses will be discussed in more detail, both in this chapter and in subsequent chapters.

Most of the income you earn must be included when you
calculate your income tax liability. Your salary or wages, roy-
alties from your autobiography, alimony you receive, pension
income, winnings from your appearance on "Jeopardy," tips,
and commissions you earn must be included when you compute your gross income. Gross income must also take into
account most investment income you earn, including dividends from stocks, nearly all interest, rental income from
real estate, and gains from the sale of investment assets.

Step Two: Calculate Adjusted Gross Income

After calculating gross income, the next step is to determine
if you are eligible to claim any of the adjustments that can
reduce the adjusted gross income you report. Adjusted gross

The maximum 28 percent tax rate on realized long-term capital gains is beneficial only if your marginal federal tax rate on
regular income is higher than 28 percent. Investors with a
marginal tax rate of 15 or 28 percent don't gain any special
benefit from the maximum rate accorded capital gains.

income (AGI) is an important measure of annual income that can affect the itemized deductions and exemptions you are able to claim. Allowable adjustments include the following:

- penalties that result from early redemption of a certificate of deposit (CD)
- contributions to an Individual Retirement Account (IRA), a Keogh plan, or a self-employed Simplified Employee Pension (SEP)
- alimony payments
- one-half of your self-employment tax
- self-employed health insurance
- certain miscellaneous adjustments

Each adjustment causes a reduction in AGI, an advantage to you because a smaller adjusted gross income means you will have a reduced amount of taxable income and less taxes to pay. As a bonus, a smaller adjusted gross income may also allow you to claim a larger amount of itemized deductions and exemptions.

Compared to the wide variety of deductions that can be used to reduce your tax liability (discussed in more detail later in this chapter), adjustments are much more restricted. Many taxpayers find they are unable to claim any adjustments that would reduce their adjusted gross income. In short, adjustments are valuable, but difficult to take advantage of.

Step Three: Calculate Taxable Income

Most taxpayers find that taxable income is the bottom line in their annual struggle with tax authorities. The more that taxable income can be reduced, the less that must be paid in

---

Figure 4

SELECTED FEDERAL INCOME TAX DEDUCTIONS

Casualty and theft losses—unreimbursed losses from natural disasters, unlawful acts, or accidents. Only losses exceeding 10 percent of adjusted gross income plus $100 can be deducted.

Charitable contributions—gifts of money or property to certain charitable organizations.

Interest—interest to finance investments including investment income, mortgage interest, interest on a home equity loan.

Job-related and miscellaneous expenses—unreimbursed employment expenses such as uniforms, union dues, travel, and continuing education, plus tax preparation fees and investment expenses. Only expenses that exceed 2 percent of adjusted gross income can be deducted.

Medical and dental expenses—physicians' fees, hospital expenses, medical insurance premiums, prescriptions, eyeglasses, hearing aids. Only expenses that exceed 7.5 percent of adjusted gross income can be deducted.

Moving expenses—expenses involved in moving to a new place of employment that is at least 35 miles farther from your former home than your old job location.

State and local taxes—state and local income taxes, real estate taxes, personal property taxes.

---

taxes. Both allowable deductions and exemptions cause reductions in the amount of taxable income you report for a given level of adjusted gross income. Deductions are particularly important and can result in thousands or even tens of thousands of dollars in tax savings. The more deductions and exemptions you are able to claim, the less taxes you will be required to pay. The amount of tax savings you are able to squeeze from deductions against income depends both on the amount of deductions and on your effective tax rate.

Currently, every dollar of usable deductions saves anywhere from 15 to 40 cents in taxes. The only exception to this relationship between taxable income and taxes owed occurs if you have tax credits, or "offsets," that can be used to reduce taxes on a dollar-for-dollar basis.

Deductions. The U.S. Congress determines what deductions individual taxpayers can use to reduce their taxable income. Allowable deductions are frequently chosen as much for political as for economic reasons. Any business, other organization, or individual that is favorably affected by a particular deduction will pursue every effort to make certain the deduction remains in the tax code. Allowable deductions have a major impact on the manner in which individuals and businesses spend money. When a particular type of expenditure is permitted as a deduction, there will be an increase in the spending associated with that deduction. Deductibility of mortgage interest causes individuals and families to spend more on houses, a result that supports real estate prices and benefits virtually everyone associated with the real estate industry. Likewise, the deductibility of charitable contributions causes increased gifts to the United Way, the Salvation Army, the Red Cross, and many other charitable organizations. These organizations consider the deductions for charitable contributions to be a very important part of the federal tax code.

When calculating taxable income, you are permitted to choose between using allowable deductions that are actually

Tax savings offset a portion of realized investment losses. The higher your tax rate, the more tax savings you will reap from a realized investment loss.

incurred or a predetermined *standard deduction* that in 1993 amounted to $3,700 for people filing individually and $6,200 for those filing jointly. The amount of the standard deduction is adjusted annually for changes in consumer prices. Choosing to use the standard deduction greatly simplifies the chore of preparing your income taxes because there is no need to maintain the records that serve as proof of your expenditures. The standard deduction is likely to offer a good deal if you haven't incurred a large amount of expenditures that would qualify for deductibility. If, for example, you had total deductions of $4,500 during 1993, you could still use the full $6,200 standard deduction to reduce your 1993 taxable income and income tax liability. In general, if you have a mortgage on your home that causes you to pay substantial amounts of mortgage interest, you are likely to have itemized deductions that exceed the standard deduction.

A recent change in the tax code requires you to use less than the full amount of your itemized deductions when your adjusted gross income exceeds a predetermined level (currently $140,000 for a joint return). Thus, individuals and families with high incomes do not receive the same benefits from deductible expenditures as do taxpayers with income below the critical level.

Tax laws are not written in stone. A tax law in effect at the time you purchase an investment may be substantially modified by the time you sell the investment. There is no certainty you will be "grandfathered" and allowed to pay taxes under the old law rather than the new law. A change in the tax code could result in higher taxes than you had anticipated at the time you purchased the investment.

Exemptions. Exemptions are special deductions you may take from adjusted gross income for just being alive and also for providing most or all of the financial support for yourself and certain other individuals (pets excluded). You are allowed to claim exemptions for yourself, your spouse, and your dependents. Dependents can include your children and other relatives who live with you or are temporarily away because of school or military service. Exemptions are different from itemized deductions in that you are not required to incur a specific expenditure in order to claim an exemption.

Congress determines the amount by which you are able to reduce taxable income for each exemption. In tax year 1993 you were entitled to an exemption of $2,350 each for you, your spouse, and other qualified dependents. With a standard deduction of $6,200 and four $2,350 exemptions, a family of four would need an annual income above $15,600 [$6,200 + (4 x $2,350)] before any federal income tax would have to be paid. A married couple without dependents could earn up to $10,900 [$6,200 + (2 x $2,350)] without being required to pay any federal income taxes.

Like itemized deductions, exemptions are subject to being reduced in size when your adjusted gross income exceeds a specific level. For tax year 1993, the exemption phaseout commenced at an adjusted gross income of $108,450 for single people and $162,700 for couples filing jointly. Clearly, you must have a substantial income not to be able to claim the full amount of each exemption.

Step Four: Calculate the Tax

Your tax liability depends on two things: the amount of your taxable income and the tax rate(s) that is (are) applied to taxable income. Low tax rates allow you to retain most of your taxable income, while high tax rates claim a larger portion of your taxable income for the government. Tax rates are periodically changed as the government's need for revenues changes and as the political philosophy of Congress and the administration shifts.

The federal income tax is *progressive*. That is, the tax is structured so that increasing amounts of taxable income are taxed at progressively higher rates. The theory behind a progressive tax is that individuals with high incomes are better able to foot the government's bills. Also, some social scientists contend that individuals and families with high incomes receive greater benefits from the goods and services that governments typically deliver.

The tax rates applied to successively greater amounts of income are known as *marginal,* or *incremental, tax rates* because the rates are applied in step-wise fashion to progressively higher blocks of income. (*Marginal* is a term revered by economists, who use it with great frequency, even in their everyday discussions.) Thus, a progressive tax system may apply a low tax rate to the first $20,000 of taxable income, a higher rate to the *next* $30,000 of income, and an even higher rate to taxable income above $50,000. If you have a taxable income of $18,000, such a tax system would cause

Don't put tax savings above all other investment goals. Tax savings are important but not so important as choosing investments with risk and return that are appropriate to your own financial situation. Investing in a very risky asset that may lose substantial value and provide you with large tax write-offs is a tough way to get wealthy.

you to pay the lowest scheduled rate on all your taxable income. With a taxable income of $40,000, your tax liability is determined by applying the lowest rate to the first $20,000 of taxable income, and the next highest rate to the remaining $20,000 of taxable income. A progressive system can include two, three, or even more applicable rates. The more rapidly tax rates are scheduled to rise as taxable income increases, the more progressive the structure of the income tax and the greater amount of the total tax bill that will be shouldered by individuals with high incomes.

Some states and municipalities with personal income taxes have chosen to levy *proportional* taxes. A proportional income tax applies the same tax rate to all incomes, regardless of size. Thus, a person with $20,000 of taxable income would face the same tax rate (but less taxes) as someone with a taxable income of $200,000, or even someone with $2 million of taxable income. Proportional tax systems are most popular in states and municipalities that levy low tax rates where there is less opportunity for an incremental system of rates. States with comparatively high income tax rates (relative to other states, but not the federal government) generally opt for a progressive tax schedule that allows taxpayers with low incomes to pay low rates.

The federal income tax currently has five marginal tax rates that range from 15 to 39.6 percent (see Figure 5). Individuals and families with modest incomes pay a single rate of 15 percent on all their taxable income. Only when the taxable income of a single individual rises above $22,100 and the taxable income of a couple filing jointly rises above $36,900 (for tax year 1993) is any income subject to a rate higher than 15 percent. A family of five or six with a large amount of deductions could earn substantially more than $36,900

Figure 5

FEDERAL INCOME TAX SCHEDULES, 1993

Single

Taxable Income	Tax
$ 0 – $ 22,100	15 percent of taxable income
22,100 – 53,500	$ 3,315 plus 28 percent over $22,100
53,500 – 115,000	12,107 plus 31 percent over $53,500
115,000 – 250,000	31,172 plus 36 percent over $115,000
More than $250,000	79,772 plus 39.6 percent over $250,000

Married Filing Jointly

Taxable Income	Tax
$ 0 – $ 36,900	15 percent of taxable income
36,900 – 89,150	$ 5,535 plus 28 percent over $36,900
89,150 – 140,000	20,165 plus 31 percent over $89,150
140,000 – 250,000	35,928 plus 36 percent over $140,000
More than $250,000	75,528 plus 39.6 percent over $250,000

Married Filing Separately

Taxable Income	Tax
$ 0 – $ 18,450	15 percent of taxable income
18,450 – 44,575	$ 2,767 plus 28 percent over $18,450
44,575 – 70,000	10,082 plus 31 percent over $44,575
70,000 – 125,000	17,964 plus 36 percent over $70,000
More than $125,000	37,764 plus 39.6 percent over $125,000

Head of Household

Taxable Income	Tax
$ 0 – $ 29,600	15 percent of taxable income
29,600 – 76,400	$ 4,440 plus 28 percent over $29,600
76,400 – 127,500	17,544 plus 33 percent over $127,500
127,500 – 250,000	33,385 plus 36 percent over $127,500
More than $250,000	77,485 plus 39.6 percent over $250,000

and still be taxed at a rate no higher than 15 percent.

The range of income subject to each rate is known as a *tax bracket*. You are in the 28 percent tax bracket if the amount of your taxable income requires you to pay a tax rate of 28 percent on the highest part of your income. Tax brackets do not remain constant. In fact, under the current law tax brackets are automatically adjusted upward when consumer prices rise, in order to keep inflation from penalizing taxpayers by allowing their inflation-caused raises to be taxed at higher rates. The two highest brackets included in Figure 5 were added to the existing three rates during the first year of the Clinton administration, when the president claimed that federal deficits were too large and that individuals with high incomes were not being asked to do their part to make the deficit smaller.

Determining your federal tax liability is relatively easy once you have calculated your taxable income. Suppose you wish to calculate the tax liability when you and your family have $70,000 of taxable income. Applying the appropriate schedule in Figure 5 for a couple filing jointly, the tax equals $5,535 plus 28 percent of income in excess of $36,900. The amount of $5,535 that is provided in the table represents the tax on the first $36,900 of taxable income. With $70,000 of taxable income, the remaining $33,100 will be taxed at 28 percent, producing a total tax bill of $5,535 +

Regardless of the tax benefits you may expect, it is generally a mistake to invest a very large proportion of your savings in one particular type of asset. For example, don't put all your savings into municipal bonds, real estate, insurance, stocks, or any other group of assets.

Figure 6

CALCULATING THE TAX LIABILITY,
MARGINAL TAX RATE, AND AVERAGE TAX RATE

Suppose you and your spouse are DINKs (double income, no kids). You have combined salaries of $62,000, $2,500 of dividend income from common stocks, and $1,500 of interest income from a money market account. The two of you rent an apartment and have few deductions causing you to use the standard deduction when computing your federal income tax liability.

A. Your federal tax liability is calculated as

$ 62,000	salaries
2,500	plus: dividend income
1,500	plus: interest income
$ 66,000	gross income
0	less: adjustments
$ 66,000	adjusted gross income
6,200	less: standard deductions
4,700	less: personal exemptions
$ 55,100	taxable income

Using tax schedule in Figure 5 for married couples filing jointly, your tax liability on $55,300 of taxable income would be:

$$\$ 5,535 + .28 \times (\$55,100 - \$36,900)$$
$$= \quad \$ 5,535 + \$5,096$$
$$= \quad \$10,631$$

B. Your marginal tax rate is 28 percent because you are required to pay 28 percent of additional income in taxes.

C. Your average tax rate is $10,631 ÷ $55,100, or 19.3 percent.

(.28 × \$33,100), or \$14,803. You could also compute the tax liability by multiplying the income applicable to each bracket by the appropriate tax rate. The tax liability calculated in this manner is:

$$
\begin{aligned}
.15 \times \$36,900 &= \$\ 5,535 \\
+ \ .28 \times \$33,100 &= \underline{9,268} \\
\text{tax liability} &= \$14,803
\end{aligned}
$$

The second method clearly illustrates that a rate of 15 percent is applied to the first \$36,900 of income and a substantially higher rate of 28 percent is applied to the next \$33,100 of taxable income. This distinction is often lost when the tax tables or tax rate schedule is used to compute your taxes.

Your *average tax rate* is equal to the total amount of tax divided by taxable income. In this instance, the average tax rate is calculated as \$14,803/\$70,000, or 21.1 percent, substantially less than the marginal tax rate of 28 percent. With a progressive tax system, the tax rate you pay on additional income (your marginal tax rate) is always higher than the tax rate you pay on all your income (your average tax rate). The average tax rate you pay is interesting to know but provides little guidance in making financial decisions.

CHAPTER 2

How Taxes Affect Your Investments

Taxes you will be required to pay on the investment income you earn should be an important consideration when you choose investments to own. Taxes you must pay on investment income reduce the money you have available to spend or reinvest and cause an investment to be less attractive. You should use after-tax income rather than before-tax income to evaluate the profitability of an investment. The difference between before-tax income and after-tax income is a function of the applicable tax rate and the proportion of income that is subject to taxation. The higher your tax rate, the more you benefit from owning investments that provide special tax breaks.

The tax consequences of owning an investment should always be in the back of your mind when you are making decisions regarding how to invest your money. At the same time, you should not become so antitax that you go to any lengths to avoid paying a portion of your investment income to the government. Financial experts are nearly unanimous in their advice that you should not make an investment decision based *only* on tax consequences. The investment scene is littered with individuals who have frittered away their money on high-risk investments that promised little other than tax savings. Taxes are important, but they are not the only or even the most important consideration in evaluating an investment.

Taxes and Investments

Personal taxes reduce the investment income you have available to spend or reinvest. Tax authorities confiscate a portion of the dividends you receive from shares of common and preferred stock you own, and from interest earned from savings accounts, certificates of deposit, and bonds that you hold. For every $100 in dividends or interest you receive, you probably surrender anywhere from $15 to $45 in taxes to federal, state, and local tax authorities. Being required to part with a portion of your investment income may cause you to have a less-than-favorable attitude toward taxes.

Taxes and Investment Value

A reduction in current investment income you have available to spend or reinvest is not the only negative aspect of taxation. Investments are valuable for the income they provide, and being required to surrender a portion of investment income to taxes has the effect of reducing the market value of an investment. If two investments provide the same annual income, but one pays income that is not taxable while the other pays income that is fully taxable, which of the two investments would you rather own? Well, every other investor would also prefer the alternative that pays tax-free income, and these investors will almost certainly pay a premium price to own it. That is, the investment that provides the same before-tax income but more after-tax income can be expected to have a higher market value.

Because investment values are negatively impacted by taxes, an increase in tax rates causes most investments to decline in market value. Conversely, a decrease in the tax rate applied to investment income increases the market value of investments. If the federal government altered the current tax code to make dividend income tax-exempt, stock prices would almost surely experience sharp increases. Likewise, removing the taxability of rental income would increase the market value of rental housing. Conversely, an increase in the tax rate applied to common stock dividends would decrease the market value of common stocks, especially stocks that investors choose primarily for the dividends they pay. The increased tax would have less effect on

Investment advisers are almost unanimous in their advice that you shouldn't let tax considerations override investment considerations. Investments should be appealing based on their investment potential, not just their potential to save taxes.

the prices of common stocks valued primarily for their growth prospects.

The previous chapter mentioned that taxes reduce the amount of money you are able to retain when you realize a gain on the sale of an investment asset. Capital gains, or increases in the market values of investment assets, are an important potential source of income to many investors. Stocks, bonds, real estate, precious metals, and many other investments fluctuate in price, thus creating the opportunity for an investor to profit from increases in market value.

Gains generally become taxable only when an investment is sold, but owning an asset that has appreciated in value means that you will eventually be confronted with a tax bill. The tax will be paid next year, or five years from now—whenever you decide to sell the investment. Thus, bonds you purchased for $9,000 three years ago may now have a market value of $10,000, but you will not be able to retain the full market value of the securities when the bonds are sold, because a part of the gain—and part of the proceeds from the sale—will be lost to taxes.

Before-Tax and After-Tax Income

Taxes consume such a large proportion of income that discussions of investment income usually distinguish between *gross (before-tax) income* and *after-tax income*. Gross income is the income you earn before any reductions for taxes. If your monthly salary is $2,000 and you earn another $4,000 in annual investment income, your annual gross income is $28,000. *After-tax income* represents the income you have available for spending and saving. Taxes levied by federal, state, and local governments can siphon

---

Figure 7

INCOME TAX ON A REALIZED INVESTMENT GAIN

Suppose several years ago you purchased 200 shares of the common stock of Union Pacific Corporation at a price of $60 per share. You recently sold the same shares at a price of $75. The transactions involved brokerage commissions of $120 to purchase the shares and $135 to sell the shares. Your gain would be calculated as

$15,000	Revenue from sale ($75 × 200)
− 135	less: commission to sell
$14,865	Proceeds from sale
$12,000	Cost of stock ($60 × 200)
+ 120	plus: commission to purchase
$12,120	Cost basis
$ 2,745	Realized gain (proceeds − cost basis)

Federal income taxes on the gain will be 28 percent of $2,745 unless you have a modest taxable income and pay a marginal tax rate of 15 percent, in which case the tax on the gain will be 15 percent of $2,745.

---

away up to half your gross income depending on a variety of factors including the amount of your annual income, the size of your family, and the state in which you reside.

Suppose you deposit $10,000 in a savings account at a financial institution that advertises an annual interest rate of 5 percent. Your account will earn interest income of $500 (5 percent of $10,000) during the first year, an amount that will be subject to taxes. If your tax rate is 25 percent, you must pay taxes of $125 on the $500 of interest income, leaving

$375 in after-tax income to be spent or saved. The truly important measure of this investment's income is the amount of money you will be able to retain after taxes are paid. An investment that promises high income may have only a nominal value if most of the income will be lost to taxes. On the other hand, an investment that promises nominal income that will be free of taxation may have substantial value. The bottom line is that determining the amount of after-tax income you expect to receive from an investment should have a strong influence on your decision to invest in it. Don't forget to include the impact of any state and local taxes that will reduce after-tax income even more. If you are also required to pay state and local income taxes of $30 and $10, respectively, on the $500 of income from your savings account, after-tax income will be reduced even further, to $335.

Calculating the After-Tax Return on an Investment

The annual rate of return earned on an investment is calculated by dividing the value of your investment into the annual income the investment is expected to produce. In most instances, the value of your investment is measured at the beginning of the period during which you plan to calculate the investment's return. If you earn $500 in a year from a $10,000 investment, the annual before-tax rate of return is $500÷10,000, or 5 percent. Annual income is usually defined to include current income (interest or dividends) plus

Preparing your own tax return makes it more likely that you will stay current on tax regulations and understand how various investment decisions impact your taxes.

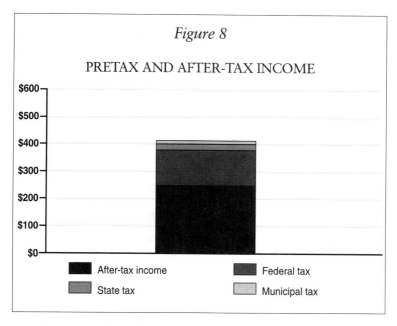

Figure 8

PRETAX AND AFTER-TAX INCOME

Legend:
- After-tax income
- Federal tax
- State tax
- Municipal tax

any change in the value of an asset, even if you don't sell the investment. Suppose you own mutual fund shares that were valued at $10,000 at the beginning of the current year. If the shares pay $300 in dividends and increase in value by $600, to $10,600, during the year, the annual before-tax rate of return earned from owning the mutual fund shares is ($300 + $600) ÷ $10,000, or 9 percent.

An investment's after-tax rate of return (rates are stated as a percentage rather than as a dollar amount) is calculated by dividing after-tax income by the amount of your investment. In equation form this is shown as

$$\text{after-tax return} = \frac{\text{investment income} - \text{taxes on income}}{\text{investment value at beginning of period}}$$

If your income is subject to a tax rate of 40 percent you will be able to retain only 60 percent of the investment income you receive. In this case, the bank savings account that pays annual interest of $500 provides after-tax spendable income of $500 less 40 percent of $500, or $300. In percentage terms this is an annual after-tax return of $300 ÷ $10,000, or 3 percent.

Annual returns are calculated somewhat differently for investments that are subject to changes in market value, such as common stocks, bonds, and real estate. For these investments market value is often substituted in the above formula for the amount invested. Suppose eight years ago you purchased one hundred shares of stock for $4,300. At the beginning of the current year, the stock was valued at $6,200 (the stock had increased in value by $1,900 during the eight years). If the stock pays a dividend of $490 in the current year, during which time it also increases in price to $7,100, the $900 gain combined with the $490 dividend would produce a return of ($900 + 490) ÷ $6,200, or 22.4 percent. This represents the before-tax return you earn on the stock.

An investment's after-tax return can also be calculated by adjusting the before-tax return by the tax rate. This is the best alternative when the before-tax return is already known and when all investment income is subject to the same tax rate. After-tax return is equal to the before-tax return times

Investments with unusually high yields generally subject an investor to substantial risk even though a salesperson may tell you otherwise. An investment with a very high yield calls for extra scrutiny on your part.

Figure 9

COMPARING AFTER-TAX RETURNS

You are selecting among three investments on the basis of the highest after-tax return. Investment 1 pays a before-tax (also called *pretax*) return of 8 percent that is taxed at your regular tax rate of 35 percent. Investment 2 has a pretax return of 6 percent that is taxed at a special rate of 15 percent. A third investment pays a tax-free return of 5 percent. Which of the three investments should you choose if you are interested only in earning the highest possible after-tax return?

Investment 1
after-tax return = .08 × (1 − .25) = 6.0 percent
Investment 2
after-tax return = .06 × (1 − .15) = 5.1 percent
Investment 3
after-tax return = .05 × (1 − .0) = 5.0 percent

You should choose investment 1 based on the fact that you will earn a higher after-tax return, of 6 percent.

---

1 minus the applicable tax rate. One minus the applicable tax rate represents the proportion of investment income you will retain after taxes have been paid. This seemingly complicated explanation actually involves a relatively simple computation. In equation form the after-tax return is

$$\text{after-tax return} = \text{before-tax return} \times (1 - \text{tax rate})$$

Using this equation, the after-tax return on the savings account paying 5 percent interest is calculated as .05 × (1 − .4), or 3 percent when your income is subject to a 40 percent tax rate. This is the same answer previously calculated using after-tax income. In this example you retained 60 percent of investment income and 60 percent of the before-tax return. It is handy to be able to convert before-tax returns to after-tax returns because investments are often quoted and compared on the basis of their rates of return, not the dollar amount of the income they provide.

Importance of the Tax Rate

Unless a particular type of investment income is subject to a special tax rate (e.g., realized capital gains), the income you are able to retain from an investment is a function of the tax rate that is applied to the highest amount of your gross income. This rate is called your *marginal tax rate* because it is applied to the additional, or marginal, income you earn. If the federal and state governments take 35 percent of each dollar of extra income you earn, your marginal tax rate is 35 percent and you will be able to keep 65 cents of each dollar you earn from investment income. You will be able to retain only 55 percent of investment income if the applicable tax rate is subsequently raised to 45 percent. A higher tax rate reduces the investment income you retain and, as a result, reduces your incentive to invest.

If all investment income were subject to exactly the same tax rate, an investment that provided a higher before-tax income would also provide a higher after-tax income. Suppose a money market account at a local bank is currently paying a return of 3.5 percent while a local savings & loan association is offering 3.8 percent on a similar account. With $5,000 to deposit in one of the two financial institutions, you calculate that the bank account will earn an annual in-

Figure 10

CALCULATING AN INVESTMENT'S
AFTER-TAX INCOME AND RETURN

You recently bought a $10,000 Treasury note that will mature in one year. The note has a 6 percent interest coupon and was purchased for its face value. You are single and have taxable income of $45,000, excluding the $600 of interest income you will earn from the note.

Using the tax schedules from Figure 5 and excluding interest on the note, your tax liability will be

$$\$3,315 + .28(\$45,000 - \$22,100)$$
$$= \$3,315 + \$6,412$$
$$= \$9,727$$

where $3,315 represents the tax due on the first $22,100 of income that is taxed at a rate of 15 percent. The calculation can also be shown as

$$.15 \times \$22,100 = \$3,315$$
$$.28 \times \underline{\$22,900} = \underline{\$6,412}$$
$$\$45,000 \qquad \$9,727$$

Thus, you will pay $9,727 in federal income taxes on income of $45,000.

Interest income of $600 from the note will be added on top of your current taxable income and taxed at your marginal tax rate of 28 percent. This means you will retain 72 percent of the $600 interest income after taxes. After-tax income from the note is calculated as

$$\$600 \ (1 - \text{marginal tax rate})$$
$$= \$600 \ (1 - .28)$$
$$= \$600 \ (.72)$$
$$= \$432$$

The after-tax return you earn on the note is calculated as the after-tax income divided by the amount of your investment. In this example, the after-tax is shown as

$$\frac{\$432}{\$10,000} = 4.32 \text{ percent}$$

The return can also be calculated by multiplying the pretax return of 6 percent times 1 minus your marginal tax rate. This is shown as:

$$6 \text{ percent } (1 - .28) = 4.32 \text{ percent}$$

come of $175 while the savings & loan account will earn an annual income of $190. If both investments are taxed at the same rate (which, in fact, they would be), the investment alternative offering the higher return before taxes will also provide the higher return after taxes. This relationship is true regardless of the size of the tax rate so long as the same rate is applied to both investments.

Suppose the investment income from each of the two investments will be subject to a 40 percent tax rate. Choosing to invest in the bank account will result in a tax of 40 percent of $175, or $70, leaving after-tax income of $105. Income from the savings & loan account will result in a tax of 40 percent of $190, or $76, leaving $114 in after-tax income. Thus, choosing to invest your $5,000 at the savings & loan will produce more income on both a before-tax and an after-tax basis.

Importance of the Type of Investment Income

A single tax rate applied to all income, regardless of the source, would make for an easy-to-understand tax code. Don't hold your breath, because simplicity is not a primary goal of tax policy and not all investment income is subject to the same tax rate. Most dividends from stocks and interest from bonds, certificates of deposit, and savings accounts are taxed at the same rate that is applied to the highest portion of your earned income. That is, you pay the same tax

Don't purchase investments by telephone from people you don't know. The world is full of people who want to grab hold of your money. Make certain you have reason to trust someone who is trying to sell you on an investment.

Figure 11

CALCULATING THE AFTER-TAX RETURN FOR AN INVESTMENT WITH INCOME TAXED AT TWO DIFFERENT RATES

Suppose that last year you purchased 500 shares of GenCorp common stock at a price of $12 per share. During the year, the stock paid a 60-cents per-share dividend, and you recently sold the stock for $15 per share, one year and a week after it was purchased. You have substantial income and pay a 36 percent tax rate on ordinary income. Because you held the stock for longer than one year, the gain is taxed at 28 percent, the maximum rate on long-term capital gains.

Calculating the after-tax return on your investment requires that you calculate the after-tax income for each component of income. Before-tax dividend income is 60 cents × 500 shares, or $300. The capital gain equals the $7,500 proceeds from the sale minus your cost of $6,000, or $1,500. Brokerage commissions, which would reduce the gain, are being omitted. The after-tax dividend income is

$$\$300 - \$300(.36) = \$300 - \$108, \text{ or } \$192$$

The after-tax gain is

$$\$1,500 - \$1,500(.28) = \$1,500 - \$420 = \$1,080$$

Total after-tax income on your investment is

$$\$192 + \$1,080 = \$1,272$$

The after-tax return on your investment is

$$\text{after-tax income/net outlay} = \$1,272/\$7,500 = 17 \text{ percent}$$

---

rate on dividend income and on most types of interest income as you pay on each extra dollar of wages or salary you earn. If your income places you in the 31 percent tax bracket (i.e., you pay 31 cents of each extra dollar of income in taxes), you will pay a tax rate of 31 percent on most types of dividend and interest income you receive. Nonetheless, not *all* sources of interest income are identical in the eyes of tax authorities. Interest income from certain investments is not subject to state taxation, while interest paid by other investments is not subject to federal taxation. Some types of interest income are not taxed at either the state or the federal level. In addition, taxes on certain types of interest income can be deferred. No one ever claimed that tax policy makes sense.

Compared to other types of income, gains that result when capital assets such as stocks, bonds, and real estate are sold at a profit have historically received a tax preference. Although the part of the tax code applicable to capital gains and losses has changed frequently over the years, capital gains are ordinarily taxed at a lower effective rate than other types of income on the theory that the reduced tax rate stimulates investment spending. Critics claim that a special rate for capital gains primarily benefits wealthy individuals, who are more likely to make large campaign contributions.

Investments that provide income subject to special low rates are in great demand, especially by investors with substantial amounts of taxable income. High-income individuals who pay high tax rates on most types of investment income are constantly on the lookout for investments with income that is taxed at relatively low rates or not taxed at all. Municipal bonds paying tax-exempt interest and investments offering potential capital gains are both prized by

Make certain to keep good records of your investment activity. The IRS or state tax authorities may require you to produce proof related to the price you paid or received for an investment.

wealthy individuals. Investments that create deductions that offset reportable income are also of interest to investors who have substantial income.

Tax Savings vs. Tax Deferral

Tax savings means that you pay a reduced amount of taxes, either because a particular type of investment income is taxed at a low rate or not taxed at all, or because only a portion of the income from a particular investment is taxable. Most municipal bonds produce tax savings for their owners because municipal bond interest is not subject to federal income taxes and may not be subject to state and local taxes. Likewise, real estate investments can produce substantial tax-deductible expenses (e.g., interest, maintenance, and depreciation) that offset income and result in tax savings. Many investments offer an opportunity to earn capital gains, which, depending on the mood of Congress, can be subject to special low rates of taxation.

Unlike tax savings, tax deferral refers to the *postponement,* or delay, of taxes, not an outright reduction in taxes. Tax deferral can actually end up costing you more in taxes because of the possibility that it may eventually result in more total income to report. You may find that tax rates are higher when your deferred income becomes taxable. Higher

Don't worry about tax-saving investments if you are in a relatively low tax bracket. Tax-saving investments often carry low yields that appeal mostly to high-income individuals who pay high tax rates.

tax rates may result from a change in the tax code or from the fact that you have greater taxable income when the deferred income is reported. On the other hand, you might find that your effective tax rate is lower at the time the deferred income becomes taxable.

Deferring taxes has the advantage of allowing you to reinvest and earn income on funds that would normally be lost to taxes. Postponing $500 of taxes enables you to put an extra $500 to work earning additional income until the tax must be paid. You will eventually be required to ante up all of those postponed taxes, of course, but only after you have had the use of funds that would otherwise be in the hands of the tax authorities. Better that you have the money for as long as possible (provided you don't squander it or lose it in a bad investment!).

The Effect of Tax Deferral

Suppose you have $50,000 invested in an asset that pays a fixed annual return of 8 percent. This investment is subject to a special tax regulation that permits you to choose whether to pay taxes currently or postpone paying taxes until you eventually sell the investment. Assume that your income from this investment will be subject to a 25 percent tax rate whenever you choose to have the income taxed. In other words, you can pay taxes currently at a rate of 25 per-

Don't purchase an investment you don't understand, no matter how good the tax consequences sound. Investing in something that is too complicated to understand means that you are more likely to be left holding the bag on a worthless investment.

cent or you can choose to defer taxes and eventually pay a tax rate of 25 percent on all the income for all the years you own the investment.

The investment pays an income of $4,000 (8 percent of $50,000) during the first year of ownership. If you decide to pay the $1,000 tax (25 percent of $4,000) at the same time you receive the investment income, $53,000 ($50,000 + $4,000 – $1,000) will be available to earn income during the subsequent period. In the second year $53,000 at 8 percent will produce $4,240 of income that will be subject to a tax of $1,060, leaving after-tax income of $3,180, and $56,180 to invest for the third year. These amounts are calculated on the assumption that you choose to pay taxes in the period the income is earned.

Suppose that you choose to defer taxes, rather than pay taxes currently. At the end of the first year, you will retain the full $4,000 of investment income that will be added to the original investment of $50,000. Income of $4,320 (8 percent of $54,000) will be earned in the second year, $80 more than the income earned in the prior example when taxes were paid currently. The bottom line to tax deferral is that the value of your investment accumulates rapidly because a greater amount of money is at work earning income. Figure 12 illustrates the annual difference at which earnings accumulate in the examples just discussed. The calculations show that deferring taxes on income will result in an investment fund that is approximately $18,000 larger after ten years compared to the account you would have if you chose to pay taxes each year. Figure 13 illustrates the buildup of an investment fund using the same assumptions, but for a period of thirty years.

Figure 12

INCREASED INVESTMENT ACCUMULATION
FROM TAX DEFERRAL

	Current Taxation			Tax Deferral	
Year	Tax Payment	Income Reinvested	Account Balance	Income Reinvested	Account Balance
1	$1,000	$3,000	$53,000	$4,000	$54,000
2	1,060	3,180	56,180	4,320	58,320
3	1,124	3,370	59,550	4,666	62,986
4	1,191	3,573	63,123	5,039	68,025
5	1,262	3,788	66,911	5,442	73,467
6	1,338	4,015	70,926	5,877	79,344
7	1,419	4,255	75,181	6,348	85,693
8	1,504	4,510	79,691	6,855	92,548
9	1,594	4,781	84,472	7,404	99,952
10	1,689	5,069	89,541	7,996	107,948

Why Tax Saving Is Preferred to Tax Deferral

Although deferring taxes causes an investment fund to experience rapid growth compared to when taxes are paid in the year income is received, the piper (read: revenuers) must eventually be paid. Deferral means that taxes are postponed, not saved. At some point you will be called upon to pay taxes on all the income that previously escaped the tax collector. Using the information in Figure 12, choosing to pay taxes currently and reinvest the remainder of your investment income allows you to accumulate $89,541 at the end of ten years. All the *income* included in this amount

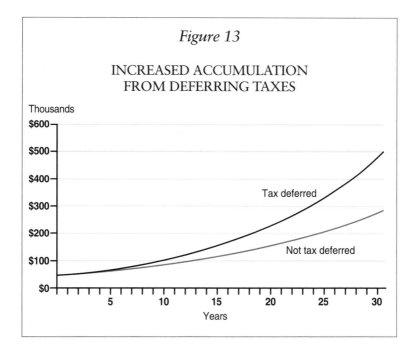

Figure 13

INCREASED ACCUMULATION
FROM DEFERRING TAXES

($89,541 less the original $50,000 investment, or $39,541) has already been fully taxed and can be withdrawn and spent without your being liable for any additional taxes. On the other hand, the $107,948 balance in the tax deferred account includes $57,948 of accumulated interest income (all the money in the account above the original $50,000) that

A loss resulting from ownership of securities that become worthless should be realized in the year the securities are declared worthless. Report the loss as if the securities were sold on the last day of the year.

Figure 14

COMPARING THE AFTER-TAX RETURNS
ON TWO INVESTMENTS

	Investment A	Investment B
Amount invested	$10,000	$10,000
Rate of return	5 percent	7 percent
Annual income	500	700
Tax @ 40 percent	0	280
After-tax income	500	420
After-tax rate of return	5 percent	4.2 percent

has never been taxed, but that must eventually be taxed when you access the funds. Assuming no change in the 25 percent tax rate, you will be required to pay a tax of $14,487 to withdraw these funds, leaving the original $50,000 investment plus $43,461 in after-tax investment income, or $93,461. Thus, choosing to defer taxes produced approximately $4,000 in additional usable funds over the ten-year period.

Now assume you could earn an 8 percent annual return that is *free of taxes*. In other words, assume that you are able to *save* taxes, not merely defer taxes. With a nontaxable return of 8 percent, your original investment of $50,000 would earn a total of $57,948 in interest income and amount to $107,948 at the end of ten years. This is the same amount available with tax deferral, except that now there are *no* taxes to pay on the income that has been earned, because all the income has been tax-free. In this example tax saving is worth $14,487 more than tax deferral.

Most investors are so eager to earn tax-free income that they will accept a significantly lower before-tax return compared to the return that is available from a taxable investment. For example, suppose you are offered a choice between two investments: Investment A is expected to provide a 5 percent annual return that is exempt from all taxes, while investment B will allow you to earn an annual return of 7 percent, all of which is taxable. You expect to be paying taxes at a rate of 40 percent of taxable income during the period of the investment, which means that you will be able to retain only 60 percent of the taxable income you earn from investment B, but 100 percent of the tax-exempt income you earn from investment A. Figure 14 provides a comparison of the two investments on an after-tax basis. Given the 40 percent tax rate, you would earn the highest after-tax return by choosing investment A. If the total amount of income you earn is so low that you don't pay any taxes, investment B would provide a higher return, on both a before-tax and an after-tax basis.

CHAPTER 3

Tax Implications of Wall Street Investments

Income earned on Wall Street investments is subject to several taxes that can reduce your after-tax return. Current income from dividends and interest is generally taxed at the marginal tax rate that is applicable to your taxable income. Certain types of dividends and interest are taxed differently or not at all. Gains in the market values of investment assets are generally not taxable until the assets are sold and the gains are realized. Realized gains in the value of investment assets that have been held for more than one year are subject to a maximum tax rate of 28 percent, even though you may pay a tax rate that is higher than 28 percent on regular taxable income. Being able to choose when a particular gain or loss is effective for tax purposes provides you with substantial flexibility regarding when taxes will be paid and, to a lesser extent, the tax rate that will be paid.

Inexperienced and conservative investors who place their savings in certificates of deposit, savings accounts, money market accounts, and U.S. savings bonds sometimes harbor a degree of envy toward fellow investors who dabble in the exotic and mysterious financial instruments offered up by Wall Street firms. The envy stems in large part from the excellent returns these "knowledgeable" investors are assumed to be earning. Timid investors are also likely to harbor the belief that Wall Street investors somehow avoid the kinds of taxes that eat away at the income earned by owners of CDs and money market accounts. Are they correct? Perhaps.

Tax Effects of Capital Gains and Losses

Capital assets you own generally affect your income tax liability only when an asset is sold for more or less than you paid originally. Selling a capital asset at a gain increases your tax liability by an amount that depends both on the amount of the gain and on the tax rate applied to the gain. Selling a capital asset at a loss decreases your tax liability. The amount of the capital loss and the applicable tax rate determine how much taxes are reduced. Your tax liability is affected by the amount of the gain or loss, not the amount of money you receive from a sale.

Capital Gains and Losses

Fees or commissions you pay to acquire a capital asset are added to the price you pay to determine the cost basis that will be used in calculating a gain or loss. If you pay a brokerage fee of $60 to purchase 200 shares of IBM stock at

Figure 15

FREE IRS TAX PUBLICATIONS
OF INTEREST TO INVESTORS

The Internal Revenue Service provides an extensive list of free publications that are of interest to investors. The following publications can be obtained by calling (800) 829–3676 or by sending a request to one of the following forms distribution centers:

Western Area Distribution Center
Rancho Cordova, CA 95743

Eastern Area Distribution Center
P.O. Box 85074
Richmond, VA 23261

Central Area Distribution Center
P.O. Box 8903
Bloomington, IL 61702

Publication

Number	Publication
526	*Charitable Contributions*
527	*Residential Rental Property*
544	*Sales and Other Dispositions of Assets*
550	*Investment Income and Expenses*
551	*Basis of Assets*
560	*Retirement Plans for the Self-Employed*
561	*Determining the Value of Donated Property*
564	*Mutual Fund Distributions*
571	*Tax-Sheltered Annuity Programs for Employees of Public Schools and Certain Tax-Exempt Organizations*
575	*Pension and Annuity Income*
590	*Individual Retirement Accounts*
909	*Alternative Minimum Tax for Individuals*
924	*Reporting of Real Estate Transactions to the IRS*
925	*Passive Activity and At-Risk Rules*
936	*Home Mortgage Interest Deduction*
1212	*List of Original Issue Discount Instruments*

$55 per share, the cost basis for the stock is (200 × $55) + $60, or $11,060. If you subsequently sell the stock for $75 per share and pay a brokerage commission of $65, net proceeds from the sale are (200 × $75) − $65, or $14,935. The gain realized on the two transactions equals the net proceeds minus the basis, or $3,875.

Now suppose the prices are reversed and you purchase 200 shares at $75 each and later sell the stock for $55 per share. Your basis for the stock is (200 × $75) + $65, or $15,065, and the net proceeds are (200 × $55) − $60, or $10,940. The realized capital loss equals the difference between the two, or $4,125.

Long-Term and Short-Term Gains and Losses

Realized gains and losses are classified as *long-term* when the asset that is sold has been owned for more than one year. Ownership for a year or less results in a gain or loss being classified as *short-term*. Holding an asset for more than a year and having a realized gain or loss classified as long-term rather than short-term are important to the extent that the holding period impacts your tax liability. If short- and long-term gains are taxed in an identical manner, there is no reason to care whether an asset is held for more than a year before it is sold. On the other hand, long-term gains should be preferred if they are taxed at a lower rate than short-term gains. A lower tax rate applied to long-term gains is likely to cause you to hang on to capital assets long enough for the gain to qualify for special tax treatment.

The tax treatment of realized capital gains and losses has varied over the years, depending on the whims of Congress. For many years prior to the tax reform enacted in 1986, only 50 percent—and, later, 40 percent—of realized long-term gains were subject to *any* taxation. Avoiding taxes on 60 percent of realized gains was a great boon to wealthy investors who sometimes paid marginal tax rates of 50 to 70 percent on other investment income.

Current law applies a maximum tax rate of 28 percent to realized long-term gains. If you have a modest income that is taxed at 15 percent, long-term gains will be taxed at the same 15 percent so long as the gains don't cause the highest part of your taxable income to jump into the next tax bracket of 28 percent. A short-term gain increases your taxable income by the amount of the gain and is taxed at whatever rate applies to your other taxable income. If your taxable income is high enough that the highest portion of the income is taxed at 31 percent, short-term capital gains will also be taxed at 31 percent. Realized capital losses, both short-term and long-term, reduce your taxable income by up to $3,000 per year. Losses greater than $3,000 must be carried forward and used to offset income in future years, when the $3,000 maximum will again apply. Losses may be carried forward indefinitely, until the losses are used up. The $3,000 annual limitation for using capital losses to offset regular income is a product of Congress, not the Internal Revenue Service.

Itemized deductions for expenditures such as interest, state and local income taxes, and charitable contributions do not result in tax savings unless the total of these deductions exceeds the amount of the standard deduction. Examine last year's tax return to determine if you are likely to itemize or to use the standard deduction in the current tax year.

Multiple Gains and Losses in the Same Year

When you sell several capital assets during the same year, you may have both gains and losses to report on your tax return. To further complicate matters, some of the gains and losses may be long-term while others are short-term. To determine the tax treatment when several assets are sold during the same year, do the following:

1. In four separate categories add all your long-term gains, long-term losses, short-term gains, and short-term losses.
2. Offset long-term gains with long-term losses, and offset short-term gains with short-term losses.
3. Depending on the results of step 2, either offset net long-term gains with net short-term losses, or offset net short-term gains with net long-term losses.

These calculations will yield one of the following outcomes:

1. A net long-term gain that is taxed at your marginal rate or 28 percent, whichever is lower.
2. A net short-term gain that increases your taxable income and is taxed at the marginal rate applicable to your ordinary income.
3. A net long-term loss that reduces your taxable income by up to $3,000 in the current tax year. Losses above $3,000 must be carried forward to offset capital gains or ordinary income in future years.

Taxes are not something to be avoided at any cost. There is a point where the risk is too high or the return is too low to justify putting your money into an investment, no matter how much tax savings you can expect to reap.

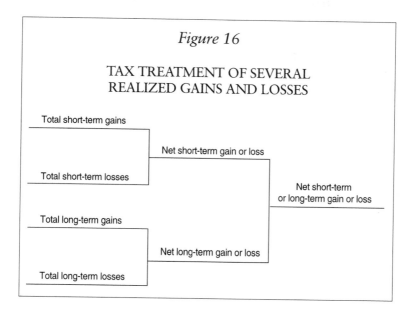

Figure 16

TAX TREATMENT OF SEVERAL
REALIZED GAINS AND LOSSES

Total short-term gains

Net short-term gain or loss

Total short-term losses

Net short-term
or long-term gain or loss

Total long-term gains

Net long-term gain or loss

Total long-term losses

4. A net short-term loss that is treated in the same manner as the net long-term loss in outcome 3.
5. A net long-term gain and a net short-term gain that are treated as described in outcomes 1 and 2.
6. A net long-term loss and a net short-term loss that are added together and used to reduce the current year's taxable income by up to $3,000. Capital losses above $3,000 must be carried forward to future years.

Not All Gains and Losses Are Taxed the Same

Not all increases and decreases in asset values are treated in exactly the manner outlined above. For example, discounts on purchases of many long-term debt instruments must be amortized (spread) over the expected life of the bond. Instead of reporting the gain in value (i.e., the difference between the face value returned at maturity and the purchase price) as a long-term capital gain at the time the security is sold or redeemed, you are required to report a portion of the discount as income each year you hold the bond. Gains originating from bonds purchased at a discount are subject to the same marginal tax rate applicable to interest income and other regular income, rather than at the special rate applicable to long-term capital gains.

Taxable bonds purchased at a discount on the date of issue (*original issue discount bonds*) also require you to pay regular tax rates on increases in value as a bond moves nearer to maturity; it will then be redeemed at face value. The larger the original discount, the more annual income you earn from scheduled increases in value compared to semiannual interest payments. Some bonds, termed *zero-coupon bonds,* have no scheduled interest payments and are sold at a deep discount from face value. The only income earned from a zero-coupon bond is the difference between the price paid and the price received when the bond is sold or redeemed.

Increases in the cash value of a life insurance policy are not subject to the long-term capital gains rate, no matter how long the policy is owned. In fact, generally no tax is

When you itemize deductions, you can often save on taxes by bunching your deductions in alternate years. Use the standard deduction in other years when few itemized deductions are available. Charitable contributions and state income taxes are often easy to bunch.

due on the cash buildup in a life insurance policy until the cash value is withdrawn by the policyholder. Even then a tax is due only when the money withdrawn exceeds the sum of the premiums that have been paid. In the event a policyholder dies, the face value of the policy is paid to the designated beneficiary and no income tax is due from either the recipient or the deceased's estate. Taxation of life insurance is covered in more detail in chapter 6.

These are only a few of many exceptions to the general rules of capital gains taxation outlined above. Taxation of rental property, futures contracts, options, bonds purchased at a premium or discount, and partnerships often involve complicated calculations that give powerful headaches to both professional and amateur tax preparers.

Tax Implications of Common Stock Investments

Common stocks are the best known and most popular of Wall Street investments. Shares of common stock represent business ownership. A small business may have no more than a few hundred shares of stock in investors' hands, while a very large corporation may have issued hundreds of millions of shares of common stock that are held by tens of thousands of investors. The more shares of stock a particular company issues, the smaller the proportional ownership each share represents. Owning 1,000 shares of the common stock of a company that has 1 million shares outstanding represents 1,000 ÷ 1,000,000, or one-tenth of 1 percent of the total ownership. Each common share ranks equally with every other share of a particular class of stock.

Of the many factors affecting the price at which a stock

is traded, none is more important than the underlying profitability of the company that issued the stock. As owners, the holders of common stock have a claim to the income a business earns after expenses have been paid. All or a portion of this income may be distributed to the firm's owners as dividends, or the income may be reinvested in additional assets that will cause the company to grow and earn even greater profits in future years. The decision regarding how much dividends to pay is determined by a company's directors, who are elected by the shareholders. In practice, directors generally choose to distribute a portion of annual earnings and reinvest the remainder.

The division of income between dividends and reinvestment is partly a function of the directors' opinions regarding the firm's reinvestment needs. A rapidly growing company that has substantial needs for additional buildings, equipment, and inventories is likely to retain all or a large portion of its profits, while an established company in a mature industry may have few investment opportunities and distribute most of its income to stockholders. Companies that retain most of their income and are able to profitably reinvest these funds offer the possibility of substantially larger earnings and dividends in future years. Growing earnings and dividends are likely to be accompanied by an increasing

Make an effort to be an informed investor. Subscribe to several business publications, even though you may not have time to read each publication in its entirety every week or month. The *Wall Street Journal* is an excellent resource for any investor. Don't waste your time and money reading books that promise to make you rich.

stock price that produces capital gains for shareholders. Firms that distribute most of their income in dividends to stockholders typically offer no better than modest growth prospects for earnings and dividends.

Taxation of Cash Dividends

Most cash dividends paid to stockholders are taxed as regular income at each stockholder's marginal tax rate. Thus, for tax purposes most dividend income is treated in the same manner as wages. Suppose you are single with a taxable income of $35,000. Using the 1993 tax schedule from Chapter 1, your tax liability is calculated as 15 percent of the first $22,100 of taxable income plus 28 percent of the next $12,900 of taxable income, or $6,927. Now suppose you also receive $1,000 in dividends during the year. Dividends add directly to your taxable income, which increases to $36,000. The added dividend income results in a tax liability of $3,315 plus 28 percent of $13,900, or $7,207, $280 above the tax before the dividend was added. The additional $280 tax on $1,000 of extra dividend income demonstrates that dividend income is taxed at an investor's marginal tax rate, which in this case is 28 percent. That is, dividend income is added to other income you earn and taxed at the rate applicable to the highest portion of your total taxable income. The marginal rate in this example is 28 percent.

With cash dividends taxable at a stockholder's marginal tax rate, investors with substantial taxable incomes pay a higher tax rate on dividends than investors with modest incomes. Someone filing a joint return with a taxable income of $150,000 pays a federal income tax rate of 36 percent on

Figure 17

PER-SHARE EARNINGS AND DIVIDENDS
FOR SELECTED COMPANIES

Company	Earnings per Share	Dividends per Share	Dividend Payout Ratio
Apple Computer	$2.45	$ .48	20%
AVNET	1.91	.60	31
Bassett Furniture	1.85	.78	42
Bird Corporation	.15	.20	133
Coca-Cola Enterprises	.20	.05	25
General Electric	5.90	2.52	43
Hitachi, Ltd.	1.60	1.01	63
Home Depot	1.30	.11	8
Honeywell	2.40	.91	38
Intel	5.20	.20	4
Neutrogena	1.10	.24	22
Scientific-Atlanta	.66	.12	18
Thor Industries	1.27	.12	9
United Stationers	1.15	.40	35
Varian Associates	2.52	.39	15
Xerox Corporation	5.10	3.00	59

dividend income, while a married investor with $25,000 of taxable income pays only a 15 percent tax rate on dividend income. The varying tax rates applicable to dividend income cause common stocks with high dividends to have a greater appeal for investors with modest incomes and low tax rates. Investors with relatively large incomes not only don't need the additional current income provided by dividends but also don't want to pay the relatively high tax rates that accompany dividend income.

Not all distributions to the holders of common stock are taxable. Companies sometimes make distributions from sources other than current and accumulated earnings. A return of capital refunds a portion of your investment and results in a decrease in the cost, or *basis,* of your shares. The decreased basis eventually results in either a larger capital gain or a smaller capital loss when the stock is sold. Thus, a distribution that is a return of capital does not result in a tax in the year the distribution is received, but it does increase the capital gains tax you are likely to pay when the stock is sold. All the dividends you have received during a year should be listed on the various Form 1099-DIVs sent to you by the companies whose stock you own.

Taxation of Stock Dividends

Directors of some (but not many) companies choose to pay dividends in additional shares of stock rather than in cash. For example, a company's directors may pay stockholders a 4 percent stock dividend, meaning that the company will send each of its stockholders an additional stock certificate for 4 percent of the shares these stockholders already own. If you hold 400 shares of common stock prior to the dividend, you will receive an additional certificate for 16 shares (4 percent of 400 shares), causing you to own a total of 416 shares of stock.

Directors of a company choose to pay dividends in shares of stock rather than cash because their firm is in need of additional equity capital. The capital may be required to pay for current operations, to repay debt, or to acquire additional assets for expanded operations. A firm that earns a high rate of return on its assets is likely to have agreement among directors, managers, and stockholders that profits should be reinvested rather than distributed as cash dividends. Some firms pay a stock dividend in addition to a nominal cash dividend. For example, a firm that earns $5.00 per share might pay a 5-cent quarterly cash dividend and also pay an annual 4 percent stock dividend.

You are unlikely to get something for nothing, especially on Wall Street. A stock dividend that results in more shares of ownership but no additional assets or income for the business that paid the dividend will cause the stock price to decline. In the previous example, suppose each of your 400 shares sold for $45 prior to the 4 percent stock dividend. The total value of your holdings amounted to 400 shares × $45, or $18,000. Following the dividend, you own 416 shares that can be expected to have the same $18,000 value, meaning that the shares should each sell at a reduced price of $18,000 ÷ 416 shares, or $43.27.

Stock distributions are taxed differently than the way cash dividends so long as you do not have a *choice* of receiving cash or additional shares of stock. Having a choice means that a stock dividend is fully taxable at your marginal tax rate in the year the stock is received. If, as is usually the case, no choice is offered, a stock dividend has

Stocks that offer high dividend yields are often poor candidates for appreciation in value. Companies that pay high dividends have little earnings left over for reinvestment that is likely to produce increased future earnings.

Figure 18

FIGURING YOUR TAX LIABILITY
ON THE SALE OF A STOCK DIVIDEND

Selling shares received as a stock dividend creates a realized gain or loss based on the proceeds of the sale compared to the cost basis of the shares that are sold. Proceeds of a sale are easily determined by subtracting selling costs (i.e., brokerage commissions) from the principal of the transaction. The cost basis of shares received as a stock dividend is somewhat more complicated to calculate. To determine your basis, divide the total cost of the original shares (generally, the amount you paid, including brokerage commissions) by the number of shares owned *after* the stock dividend.

Suppose in 1992 you purchased 500 shares of General Motors common stock at a price of $40 per share. A brokerage commission of $150 caused your cost basis to equal ($40 × 500 shares) + $150, or $20,150. Two years following the date of purchase, General Motors declared a 6 percent stock dividend, causing your total holdings to increase by 30 shares, to a total of 530 shares. The cost basis of your shares, including both the original shares and the additional shares received as a result of the stock dividend, is $20,150 ÷ 530 shares, or $38.02 per share. If you subsequently sell the 30 shares from the stock dividend at a price of $65 and pay a sales commission of $35, your gain will be computed as

$ 1,950.00	principal from sale (30 shares @ $65)
− 35.00	less: commission on sale
$ 1,915.00	net proceeds from sale
	less: cost basis of shares sold
− 1,140.60	(30 shares @ $38.02)
$ 774.40	realized gain and amount subject to tax
x .28	applicable marginal tax rate
$ 216.83	tax on gain

certain tax advantages over a cash dividend. First, no income tax is due on a distribution of stock until the shares are sold, which may be many years after the dividend is received. Being able to determine when a gain or loss is realized allows you to choose the year of taxation, a potentially valuable option. You may wish to hold shares received as dividends until other realized gains or losses are available to offset the gain or loss realized on the stock dividend.

Another advantage to a stock dividend over a cash dividend is the 28 percent maximum tax rate applicable to any long-term gain you realize on the sale of the shares received as a stock dividend. For the gain to qualify as long-term, you must hold the stock for more than a year from the date the stock dividend was declared. The cap on the tax rate is a valuable benefit for shareholders who pay a marginal tax rate that is above the maximum long-term capital gains rate. Stockholders with modest incomes taxed at 15 percent do not benefit from the maximum rate applicable to long-term gains, because they will pay a tax rate lower than 28 percent.

Taxation of Automatically Reinvested Dividends

Dividend reinvestment plans (DRIPs) allow you to instruct the company whose stock you own to automatically reinvest your dividends in additional shares of stock, generally at no expense to you. Shares purchased with your dividends are credited to an account maintained by a trustee, generally a commercial bank. You don't receive an additional stock certificate each quarter, but you can always request that the trustee send a certificate for a portion or all of the shares that have been credited to your account. You can also instruct the trustee to sell some or all of the shares and send you a check for the proceeds. Another option is to have the trustee transfer a portion of your shares to another individual.

A dividend paid on the shares you own that is used to purchase additional shares of stock in a dividend reinvestment plan is fully taxable in the year the dividend is paid, even though you don't actually receive any cash. A DRIP does not save taxes by converting regular income to capital gains; neither does it defer taxes from the year the dividend is paid to the year the shares are sold (as does a stock dividend). Some companies offer the added incentive of allowing shareholders to purchase shares at a discount from their fair market value. For example, a company may allow shareholders enrolled in its DRIP to purchase additional shares at 98 percent of market value. Any discount you receive on the purchase of new shares must be reported as additional dividend income in the year the shares are purchased.

Even though no tax savings are achieved, dividend reinvestment plans allow you to increase your investment in a company at low cost. Most plans allow you the option of making extra cash contributions that purchase additional shares.

Tax Implications of Bond Investments

Bonds represent debt of the issuer, which may be a business, a city, a state, the U.S. government, or even a foreign country. As a bondholder, you are a lender to the issuer, which is required to pay regular interest (on most bonds) and eventually repay the principal of the loan. Changes in market rates of interest affect the market value of a bond that pays a fixed amount of annual interest. The longer the time until a bond matures, the greater the price fluctuations of the bond in response to changes in market interest rates. Although changes in bond values allow investors to earn capital gains and suffer capital losses, most bonds are purchased for the interest income they provide rather than for potential changes in value.

Taxation of Interest

Interest payments from corporate, foreign, and U.S. government bonds are fully taxable at your applicable marginal tax rate. In this respect, bond interest is taxed in the same manner as common stock dividends. The higher your taxable income, the higher the tax rate that will be applied to the interest income you earn. Suppose you are single with a taxable income of $52,100. Using the tax schedule in Chapter 1, your federal income tax would be calculated as $3,315 plus 28 percent of $30,000, or $11,715. Now suppose you earn additional interest income of $3,000, causing your taxable income to climb to $55,100. The $3,000 in interest income causes you to pay a tax rate of 28 percent on the first $1,400 and 31 percent on the remaining $1,600.

Interest income earned from bonds of the U.S. government is generally free from state taxation but not federal taxation.

Tax-advantaged investments are often accompanied by unusually high fees, commissions, or other costs. Sellers justify high fees by arguing that tax-advantaged investments take more effort to sell, partly because these investments are so difficult for investors to understand. Always determine the fees you must pay to acquire, hold, and sell an investment.

This feature is unimportant if you live in a state that has no personal income tax, such as Florida or Nevada. On the other hand, if you reside in New York or California, states that tax personal income at relatively high rates, this tax-saving feature of U.S. government bonds is a major benefit.

Interest income from most bonds issued by states, cities, counties, and public districts is free from federal taxation and is also often exempt from state and local income taxes. Municipal bonds remain one of the premier tax-saving investments available to individual investors. Chapter 4 is devoted exclusively to an examination of these unique securities.

Taxation of Bonds Purchased at a Premium or Discount

Interest is the only taxable income for an investor who purchases at face value a bond that is held to maturity. With no realized gain or loss, only interest is taxable. When bonds are purchased above or below face value the tax ramifications are more difficult to determine. In general, a premium or discount is amortized over the life of the bond. Amortized premiums offset interest income and reduce the bondholder's annual taxable income. Amortized discounts are added to regular interest income and cause an increase in taxes each year a bond is owned.

Tax Implications of Mutual Fund Investments

Mutual funds are investment companies operated by professional portfolio managers who invest shareholders' money in common stocks, preferred stocks, corporate bonds, mu-

---

Figure 19

AMORTIZING THE PREMIUM
FOR A BOND PURCHASED ABOVE FACE VALUE

Suppose a $1,000 par corporate bond with an 8 percent coupon was issued at par in 1980. The bond had an original maturity of twenty-five years. Market rates of interest declined during the years following the issue, causing the bond to increase in price. In 1995 you purchase this bond for $1,150. You agree to pay a large premium because new bond issues have coupons substantially below 8 percent. If you hold the bond to maturity, you will receive $1,000, resulting in a $150 capital loss.

For tax purposes, the certain loss is amortized over the ten years you expect to hold the bond. The annual amortized loss is $150 ÷ 10 years, or $15 per year. The $15 annual loss is used to offset $15 of the $80 in annual interest income, resulting in additional taxable income of $65 in each of the ten years.

An alternative method for calculating the tax is to wait and realize the entire $150 loss during the year of maturity, when the face value is returned. This is nearly always a poor choice of accounting for the loss because you must wait until maturity before you are able to offset other income. In general, you should choose to realize losses as soon as possible, since a dollar saved today is worth more than a dollar saved in the future.

---

nicipal bonds, Treasury securities, and/or a host of other financial assets. Some mutual funds specialize in certain types of investments. For example, one mutual fund may invest only in tax-exempt bonds. Another fund may invest only in the shares of companies that are judged to possess good growth potential. Still another mutual fund may oversee a diversified portfolio that contains both bonds and stocks.

Investments owned by mutual funds provide the funds with the same types of income that are earned by individual investors. Funds that invest in bonds earn interest income and funds that specialize in common stock investments earn dividend income. Both types of mutual funds realize capital gains and losses as securities in their portfolios are sold or redeemed at prices different from those paid when the securities were acquired. Mutual funds also accrue *paper profits and losses* when securities change in market value but continue to be held. Changes in the market values of securities held in a mutual fund's portfolio cause a change in the value *(net asset value,* or *NAV)* of the fund's shares. Thus, you may pay $14.50 for shares of a mutual fund that subsequently increase to $19.00 per share because of increases in the market value of the fund's portfolio. Distributions to shareholders reduce the amount of assets owned by a mutual fund and cause a decline in the price of the fund's shares.

Taxes Paid by a Mutual Fund Shareholder

Mutual funds are subject to special rules of taxation that permit the companies to avoid taxes on the income they earn from interest, dividends, and capital gains so long as this income is distributed to the funds' shareholders, who are required to report and pay taxes on the distributions. Thus, taxes on the income earned and distributed by a mutual fund depend on the tax rates applicable to each of the fund's shareholders, not on the tax rate of the fund, which is zero.

Interest and dividend income earned by a mutual fund and passed through to the fund's stockholders is taxed to

Remember that the IRS holds you responsible for the information on your tax return even when you have paid a professional to complete the return.

the stockholders at the respective marginal rates applicable to their ordinary income. Tax-exempt interest earned by mutual funds that invest in municipal bonds is passed through to mutual fund shareholders as tax-exempt income. An investor's marginal tax rate is applicable to distributions of short-term capital gains. Distributions of long-term gains (gains on securities held by a fund for more than one year) are subject to the 28 percent maximum tax rate that is applicable to gains from the sale of other capital assets. Mutual fund shareholders with modest incomes and low effective tax rates pay this same low rate on capital gains distributions. Likewise, gains realized from the sale of mutual fund shares are treated as long-term or short-term, depending on the length of time the shares have been held.

Gains from the sale of mutual fund shares are not always easy to calculate, especially when small numbers of shares have been accumulated at varying prices over an extended period of time, and less than the full amount of shares are sold. Suppose you have been accumulating shares of a mutual fund over the last dozen years. If you decide to sell half your holdings, which shares are you selling? Your tax liability may be much different depending on whether the shares acquired earliest are sold first or last. Actually, there are several ways to account for the cost basis of shares that are sold. You can average the cost of all the shares you have accumulated, you can assume the first shares bought are the first shares sold (first in, first out), or you can sell selected shares (usually the ones with the highest cost). Remember, realized gains and losses on mutual fund shares are classified as short-term or long-term based on whether the shares have been held for more than one year.

CHAPTER 4

Municipal Bonds: The Ultimate Tax Savers

Municipal bonds represent outstanding debts of states, cities, and other public subdivisions. Most, but not all, municipal bonds pay interest that is exempt from federal income taxes. This interest is also often exempt from state and local taxes. Municipal bonds are primarily of interest to investors who pay high marginal tax rates. A relatively small proportion of municipal bonds pay taxable interest or interest that is subject to the alternative minimum tax. Municipal bonds can be purchased through nearly any brokerage company. Tax-exempt income is also available to owners of unit trusts and of investment companies that hold portfolios of municipal bonds.

Municipal bonds have become a favorite investment of individuals who seek to reduce their tax bills. States, cities, and counties have accommodated this demand by annually issuing tens of billions of dollars in new tax-exempt bonds that finance the construction of roads, schools, bridges, hospitals, recycling centers, water systems, and a variety of other projects. Tax reform that took effect in 1986 closed numerous tax loopholes but left municipal bonds as one of the few tax-advantaged investments available to individuals. Subsequent increases in federal income tax rates paid by individuals and families with high taxable incomes created additional demand for tax-exempt bonds. Does all this investor interest in earning tax-exempt income from ownership of municipal bonds mean that you should be investing in these securities? Perhaps.

Fundamentals of Municipal Bonds

Municipal bonds are issued by states, cities, counties, school districts, and other public authorities that borrow funds to pay for buildings, equipment, and a host of other needs. An investor who owns municipal bonds is a lender, or creditor, to the organizations that issue the bonds. If you invest in bonds issued by the state of North Dakota, you become a

Cashing a U.S. savings bond for more than you paid creates interest income that is taxed at your marginal federal tax rate. Fortunately, interest on a savings bond is not taxed at the state and local levels, a factor that can result in significant savings depending on your state of residence.

creditor of that state. For allowing the state to use your money, you receive semiannual interest payments and the eventual return of the money you loaned. The higher the interest rate a state or municipality must pay to borrow money (i.e., to sell bonds), the more interest income you will earn as a holder of municipal bonds.

Coupon Rates and Face Values

Municipal bonds are virtually identical to corporate bonds issued by businesses and to government securities issued by the U.S. Treasury. Each bond represents money borrowed by an issuer who pledges to repay the principal amount of the debt (also called the *face value* or *par value)* to whoever owns the bond on the specified maturity date. In return for use of the lender's money, the borrower promises to pay the lender a specific amount of annual interest in equal semiannual payments. The periodic interest paid on a particular bond is determined both by the bond's principal amount and by the coupon interest rate. A $10,000 principal amount bond with a 7 percent coupon pays $350 in semiannual interest ($700 per year) for as long as the bond remains outstanding. Interest payments cease on the date the bond is redeemed and the principal amount is returned to the bondholder. The interest payment dates and the maturity date on which a bond is to be redeemed are both established at the time the bond is issued.

Municipal bonds are nearly always issued in $5,000 denominations, meaning that these securities are bought and sold in $5,000 minimums and $5,000 multiples above that. The $5,000 denomination compares to $1,000 denominations for most corporate and U.S. Treasury bonds and to

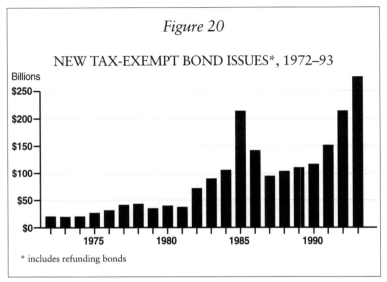

Figure 20

NEW TAX-EXEMPT BOND ISSUES*, 1972–93

Billions

$250

$200

$150

$100

$50

$0

1975   1980   1985   1990

* includes refunding bonds

$10,000 denominations for U.S. Treasury bills. You cannot ordinarily invest as little as $1,000 or $2,000 directly in municipal bonds, although you can acquire indirect ownership of these securities by purchasing shares of investment companies or unit investment trusts that hold municipal bonds. Both alternatives are addressed later in this chapter. Individual investors with modest funds are effectively priced out of the market for individual municipal bonds because of the large minimum investment that is required.

The Tax Exemption

Most municipal bonds pay interest that is not included in a bondholder's taxable income. Investing $50,000 in a 6-percent coupon municipal bond will yield $3,000 in annual tax-exempt interest income. The tax exemption applies to federal income taxes and, often, to state and local taxes as well. Interest payments to you as the holder of a municipal bond are not reported to the Internal Revenue Service by either the borrower or your broker. You are required to list on Form 1040 the amount of tax-exempt interest you receive, although this entry is for information purposes (the IRS wants to determine how much in tax revenues it is losing because of the exemption of municipal interest) and does not affect your tax liability.

Interest received from a municipal bond may or may not be taxable by the state in which you reside. Most states do not tax the interest paid by municipal bonds issued within the respective states. For example, the state of Georgia does not tax interest income from municipal bonds issued by the cities of Atlanta or Savannah (or any other Georgia city or town), or by school districts within the state. On the other hand, Georgia does tax interest income its residents receive from municipal bonds issued outside the state. Residents of Georgia must include on their state tax return interest income earned from bonds issued by the city of San Francisco or the state of Texas, for example. A few states do not tax municipal bond interest, regardless of where the bonds have been issued, and several other states tax all municipal bond interest, including interest from bonds issued in those particular states.

Even high-quality municipal bonds can be a risky investment if the bonds have long maturities and you have to sell the securities prior to maturity. Changes in market rates of interest cause major price changes in long-term bonds, meaning that you may find it necessary to sell your bonds when interest rates are high and bond prices are low.

A limited number of municipal bonds pay taxable interest. Not surprisingly, these debt securities are called *taxable municipal bonds*. The Tax Reform Act of 1986 produced this new classification when additional restrictions were established for new issues of tax-exempt municipal bonds. Municipal bonds issued to finance restricted projects—such as sports stadiums and convention centers—pay interest that does not qualify for tax-exempt status, at least at the federal level. Interest income from taxable municipal bonds often remains tax-exempt at the state and local levels.

The tax exemption of municipal bonds applies only to interest income and not to capital gains you may earn from selling these bonds at a higher price than you paid. Purchasing a long-term municipal bond at par value and later selling the bond at a premium results in a realized gain that will be taxed by the federal government. Ownership of municipal bonds can also result in realized losses when bonds are sold for less than their purchase price. Realized gains and losses in the value of municipal bonds (assuming the bond wasn't purchased at a discount or a premium) are treated for tax purposes in the same manner as gains and losses in corporate bonds and common stock.

Types of Municipal Bonds

Several methods are used to classify different types of municipal bonds. One common classification is to identify the type of guarantee that is provided to bondholders by an issuer. Municipal bonds that are fully guaranteed by the issuer are known as *general obligation bonds*, or *GOs*. The general obligation bond of nearly any state is perceived by creditors as being very safe to own, because the issuing state places its full taxing authority behind payment of the bond. The high credit quality accorded to general obligation bonds of states indicates that investors have great confidence that all the interest payments and eventual repayment of principal will occur on the scheduled dates. Not all GOs are of high quality, however. The general obligation bonds of a city or county that has become an economic basket case would have poor credit quality even with the full guarantee of repayment. On the other hand, general obligation bonds issued by financially strong states, such as Minnesota, Georgia, and Texas, are considered by the investment community to have very high credit quality.

Municipal bonds guaranteed only by the funds generated from a particular project are termed *revenue bonds*. The credit quality of a municipal revenue bond depends on the economic soundness of the project that provides the funds for repayment. Projects typically funded by municipal revenue bonds include toll roads, water and sewage systems, toll bridges, and recycling projects. If a project financed with revenue bonds proves unsuccessful (e.g., a toll road yields little revenue because drivers choose alternative routes), interest payments may cease and bondholders stand to lose all or a portion of their investment. Revenue bonds ordinarily do not have as high a credit quality as general obligation bonds, although the comparative quality can vary substan-

---

Municipal bonds should not be bought for tax-deferred retirement plans (e.g., IRAs or Keogh plans), since interest that would normally be tax-exempt will become taxable when funds are withdrawn at retirement.

tially from one bond issue to the next. Some revenue bonds are regarded as very high-quality debt obligations.

The different types of municipal revenue bonds sold to investors are usually categorized according to the type of project being financed. Municipal revenue bond categories include hospital revenue bonds, water and sewer revenue bonds, airport revenue bonds, housing authority mortgage revenue bonds, industrial revenue bonds, and electric utility revenue bonds. Among these, water and sewer revenue bonds are generally considered high-quality investments because of the essential service provided to customers. Hospital revenue bonds tend to subject bondholders to substantial amounts of risk because many hospitals are plagued with large amounts of bad debts, delayed and uncertain insurance reimbursements, and poor management.

How Municipal Bonds Are Issued and Traded

Municipal bonds are issued by states, cities, and other public subdivisions with the assistance of private investment banking firms that provide essential financial and marketing advice. Investment bankers generally also serve as underwriters, meaning that these firms purchase the issuer's bonds, which are then immediately resold to individual and institutional investors. For example, an investment banker might agree to purchase bonds from the issuer at a price of

Become familiar with bond ratings if you plan to invest in municipal bonds or tax-exempt bond funds. In general, you should limit your investments to bonds rated A and above.

$4,950 and then attempt to resell the same bonds to investors for $5,000. The difference between $5,000 and $4,950 represents the underwriter's *spread* for accepting the risk of finding buyers for the bonds.

Municipal bonds can be transferred, meaning that ownership can be assigned to another investor. You can purchase a municipal bond on Monday and resell that same bond later the same day, the following week, or ten years down the road. The issuer doesn't care how frequently its bonds are transferred so long as there is an accurate record of the owners. The issuer must know who is to receive the semiannual interest payments and, eventually, the principal.

Buying Municipal Bonds as Part of a New Issue

You must normally purchase municipal bonds that are part of a new issue from investment bankers that underwrite the issue or from brokerage firms that are able to tap into an underwriter's allocation. If you plan to purchase new issues of municipal bonds, it is helpful to maintain an account at a brokerage firm or bank that is active in bringing new municipal bond issues to market. The more new issues a firm handles, the more likely you will be able to acquire a bond with the particular characteristics you desire. Inform the broker of your interest in acquiring municipal bonds, including any preferences you have regarding maturity length, credit quality, and a specific issuer. The better the broker understands the type of bonds you are interested in purchasing, the less you will be bothered by calls about new issues in which you have little interest.

A new municipal bond issue typically comprises bonds with a wide range of maturities. It is not unusual for a single

Figure 21

COVER PAGE FROM
A MUNICIPAL BOND OFFERING STATEMENT

NEW ISSUES

$194,700,000
Georgia Development Authorities
(Oglethorpe Power Corporation Projects)

$26,785,000	$155,610,000	$12,305,000
Development Authority of	Development Authority of	Development Authority of
Appling County (Georgia)	Burke County (Georgia)	Heard County (Georgia)
Pollution Control Revenue Bonds	Pollution Control Revenue Bonds	Pollution Control Revenue Bonds
(Oglethorpe Power Corporation	(Oglethorpe Power Corporation	(Oglethorpe Power Corporation
Hatch Project),	Vogtle Project),	Wansley Project),
Series 1993	Series 1993B	Series 1993

Dated: February 1, 1994   Due: January 1, as shown below

    The 1993 Bonds of each Authority are limited obligations of such Authority payable from and secured by a pledge of revenues derived by such Authority under a Loan Agreement and a Note and by other funds pledged under a PCB Indenture. The 1993 Bonds and the interest thereon shall not be deemed to constitute a debt or general obligation or a pledge of the faith and credit of the State of Georgia or any political subdivision thereof, including Appling County, Burke County and Heard County. The obligation to make payments due to each Authority under its Loan Agreement is evidenced by a Note, which is secured on a parity basis by a first mortgage lien on substantially all of the owned tangible and certain of the intangible assets of

Oglethorpe Power Corporation

    The 1993 Bonds are issuable as fully registered bonds in the denomination of $5,000 or any integral multiple thereof. Principal and premium (if any) due on the 1993 Bonds, whether at maturity, upon redemption or otherwise, will be payable at Trust Company Bank, Atlanta, Georgia, as trustee, and semiannual interest (January 1 and July 1, 1994) due on the 1993 Bonds will be payable by check mailed on each interest payment date to the registered owner on the record date next preceding such interest payment date. The 1993 Bonds are subject to optional and extraordinary redemption as described herein.

    The 1993 Bonds of each Authority are separate issues, but contain substantially the same terms and provisions. The Underwriter reserves the right to confirm orders on any issue of the 1993 Bonds issued by any of the Authorities on an interchangeable basis at the discretion of the Underwriter.

In the opinion of King & Spalding, Bond Counsel, under existing law, and based upon certain representations, certifications and assumptions described herein under "TAX EXEMPTION," interest on the 1993 Bonds (i) is not includable in gross income for federal income tax purposes, except for any period during which such 1993 Bonds are held by a person who is a "substantial user" of the facilities refinanced thereby or a "related person" as defined in the Internal Revenue Code, and (ii) is not an item of tax preference for purposes of the federal alternative minimum tax imposed on individuals and corporations, subject to certain conditions and limitations and assuming compliance after the date of issuance of the 1993 Bonds with certain covenants as described herein under "TAX EXEMPTION." See "TAX EXEMPTION" herein for a description of certain other possible tax consequences arising with respect to the 1993 Bonds. Under existing law, and based upon certain representations, certifications and assumptions described herein under "TAX EXEMPTION," interest on the 1993 Bonds is exempt from present State of Georgia income taxation.

AMOUNTS, MATURITIES, INTEREST RATES AND PRICES

Amount	Maturity	Interest Rate	Price	Amount	Maturity	Interest Rate	Price
$10,310,000	1995	2.90%	100%	$19,795,000	2005	4.80%	100%
10,390,000	1996	3.30	100	19,775,000	2006	4.90	100
10,685,000	1997	3.55	100	19,705,000	2007	5	100
7,390,000	1998	3¼	100	11,295,000	2008	5.05	100
7,630,000	1999	3.95	100	5,510,000	2009	5.10	100
8,905,000	2000	4.15	100	870,000	2010	5.15	100
10,430,000	2001	4.35	100	2,035,000	2011	5.20	100
11,925,000	2002	4½	100	2,140,000	2012	5¼	100
15,880,000	2003	4.60	100	2,690,000	2013	5¼	100
17,340,000	2004	4.70	100				

(Accrued interest to be added)

Each issue of the 1993 Bonds will be offered when, as and if issued by the related Authority and received by the Underwriter, subject to the unqualified approving opinion of King & Spalding, Bond Counsel. Certain legal matters will be passed upon for the Underwriter by Mudge Rose Guthrie Alexander & Ferdon, Counsel to the Underwriter. Certain legal matters will be passed upon for Oglethorpe by Charles T. Autry, Esq., its General Counsel, and by Sutherland, Asbill & Brennan, Counsel to Oglethorpe. It is expected that the 1993 Bonds in definitive form will be ready for delivery in New York, New York, on or about February 23, 1994.

Smith Barney Shearson Inc.

February 3, 1994

bond issue to contain bonds with consecutive maturities for each of twenty years plus additional bonds with maturities of twenty-five and thirty years. Thus, a municipal bond issue that is brought to market in 1996 might contain bonds with maturities that begin in 1997 and run through 2026. The wide range of maturities available in most new municipal bond issues is a benefit because you can choose a bond with a maturity that best serves your needs.

Several other advantages accrue to investors who buy municipal bonds as part of a new issue. Newly issued bonds are often, but not always, sold at face value. Buying a bond at face value makes it easy to keep track of your paper profit or loss on an ongoing basis. Buying bonds that are part of a new issue also frees you from worrying about whether you should be amortizing a discount over the period you hold the bond. Discounts on municipal bonds purchased on the issue date are not considered taxable income. Likewise, premiums paid on the issue date do not result in realized capital losses. Last but not least, investors who purchase municipal bonds at the time of original issue do not pay a sales fee. The fee is absorbed by the issuer.

Buying Municipal Bonds in the Secondary Market

Investors who purchase municipal bonds that are part of a new issue frequently sell the bonds prior to maturity. Some investors with short-term goals have no intention of holding municipal bonds until maturity. Other investors may find it necessary to liquidate bonds before maturity because they need the money. The market in which previously issued municipal bonds are traded comprises many independent dealers scattered across the country. (A few municipal bond issues trade on the New York Stock Exchange.) These dealers buy municipal bonds from individuals, institutions, and other dealers, at the same time that they offer municipal bonds for sale to these same groups. Dealers act as market makers who attempt to earn a profit by reselling bonds at a slightly higher price than they pay.

You must normally go through a municipal bond dealer to purchase previously issued municipal bonds. (Many large commercial banks and brokerage companies are active municipal bond dealers.) Although a dealer can contact other dealers to search for a particular bond that meets your investment requirements (maturity, issuer, amount, etc.), most dealers offer the bonds that happen to be in their inventory at the time of your call. A particular dealer will sometimes have a large inventory of municipal bonds and be able to offer you bonds with a wide range of maturities, credit quality, and issuers. At other times a dealer will have a relatively small inventory and offer a limited selection of bonds.

Purchasing bonds in the secondary market, especially in small amounts, can be risky because you may end up paying too high a price. Unless you constantly monitor the market and spend considerable time and effort contacting different dealers while searching for the best deal, you could be overcharged without even realizing it. Bonds that are part of a

---

Long-term interest rates are normally higher than short-term interest rates. Thus, municipal bonds with long maturities will generally offer higher returns than short-term and intermediate-term municipal bonds. On the negative side, long-term bonds are subject to greater price fluctuations than short-term bonds.

new issue are sold to all investors, both big and small, at the same price, but bonds in the secondary market are sold at whatever price dealers can get.

The Risks of Owning Municipal Bonds

Municipal bonds have historically been considered high-quality investments that could be purchased with confidence that interest and principal would be paid in full and on schedule. Unfortunately, some municipal borrowers have been unable to handle their finances any better than businesses and individuals who overspent and overborrowed during the 1980s and 1990s. Even municipal bonds from financially responsible issuers can entail certain risks that investors may sometimes overlook.

Credit Risk

Credit risk for a municipal bondholder refers to the possibility that there will be a deterioration in the financial soundness of the issuer. A state, a county, a city, or, particularly, a public project can suffer economic decline, causing concern among members of the financial community that the terms of a bond issue will not be fulfilled. If residents of a specific geographic region suffer high unemployment and seek jobs elsewhere, investors holding bonds issued by cities and counties within the region are likely to be concerned about the ability of these borrowers to service their debt obligations. Even financially strong cities, counties, and states can suffer serious economic setbacks that cause creditors to experience some concern about repayment.

Figure 22

MUNICIPAL BOND QUALITY RATINGS

Standard & Poor's	Moody's	Meaning
AAA	Aaa	High grade with strong capacity for repayment
AA	Aa	High grade but slightly lower margins of protection
A	A	Medium grade with favorable attributes but susceptibility to adverse economic conditions
BBB	Baa	Medium grade but lacking certain protection against adverse economic conditions
BB	Ba	Speculative with moderate protection in an unstable economy
B	B	Speculative with small assurance of principal and interest
CCC	Caa	Poor quality in default or in danger of default
CC	Ca	Highly speculative
C		Extremely poor investment quality
	C	Making no interest payments
D		Default with interest in arrears

A deterioration of financial strength is likely to cause a decline in the value of the borrower's debt. The prices of the district's outstanding bonds are likely to take a tumble when investors become concerned that a school district will be unable to meet its financial obligations. Thus, you may realize an unexpected loss if you find it necessary to sell the municipal bonds of a city, county, or state that has experienced economic setbacks.

Interest Rate Risk

Market rates of interest are the driving force behind the market values of bonds that trade in the secondary market. Suppose you purchase at par a $5,000 principal amount, 6 percent coupon municipal bond that has a twenty-year maturity. Five years later, interest rates on new bonds of similar risk and maturity (your bond now has fifteen years to maturity) are yielding 8 percent. With the increase in market interest rates, your bond will have experienced a significant decline in price. If you continue to hold the bond to maturity, you will still have the face value returned. If, however, you decide to sell the bond because you need the money for a down payment on your dream house, the purchase of a new car, or whatever, you will receive less than you paid. No one is going to pay face value for a bond that pays $60 of interest per $1,000 face value when newly issued bonds are paying $80 per $1,000 face value.

The price volatility of a bond in response to changes in market interest rates is a function of the bond's maturity. The longer the time until a bond is to be redeemed, the more the bond will vary in value for a given change in interest rates. Short-term bonds with maturities of several years or less exhibit relatively small price movements when market interest rates change. Municipal bonds with maturities of fifteen years or more can move upward and downward in price by 15 to 20 percent or more. A long-term bond sticks you with fixed semiannual interest payments for many years. These fixed payments are to your advantage if market

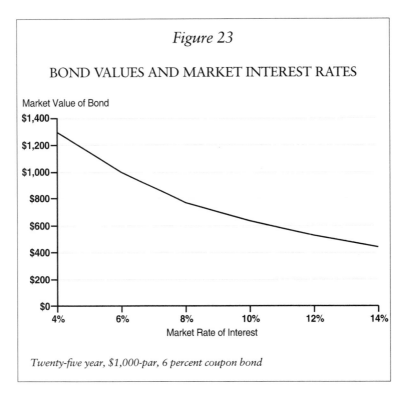

Figure 23

BOND VALUES AND MARKET INTEREST RATES

Twenty-five year, $1,000-par, 6 percent coupon bond

interest rates subsequently decline, but they will cause a decrease in the value of the bond if interest rates increase.

Purchasing Power Risk

An investment that guarantees a stream of fixed cash payments subjects an investor to substantial risk that the payments will become increasingly less valuable because of increases in consumer prices. Receiving several thousand dollars' worth of current tax-exempt interest income is one

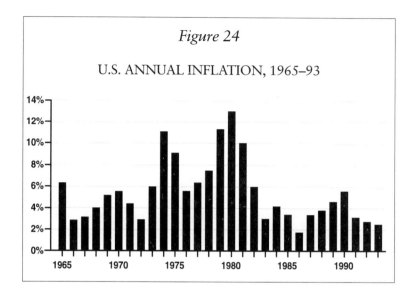

Figure 24

U.S. ANNUAL INFLATION, 1965–93

thing, but receiving the same amount of interest income fifteen or twenty years from now is likely to be much less beneficial, because of substantially higher consumer prices. If recent history is any guide, the United States can expect annual inflation of 3 to 4 percent, even in the *best* of circumstances.

Purchasing power risk is greatest when you commit your funds at a fixed interest rate for a long period of time. The interest you earn from municipal bonds or any other loan is influenced by the inflation rate both you and the borrower expect to occur over the life of the loan. The greater the inflation you both anticipate, the higher the interest rate you are likely to negotiate on a loan. If the actual inflation rate turns out to be much lower than either of you anticipated, you will benefit as a lender because the dollars of interest and principal will have greater purchasing power than you expected when the terms of the loan were determined. If inflation turns out to be much worse than expected, you will lose as a lender because the purchasing power of the cash payments from the borrower will be worth much less than you anticipated when you made the loan (i.e., bought the bond).

Liquidity Risk

At any particular time many thousands of municipal bond issues are outstanding. Some of these bonds trade actively, while other bonds may not trade for months at a time. Inactive bonds are often part of small issues. Few investors own these bonds (there aren't many bonds to own), and there is a lack of trading. Certain municipal bond issues are purchased mostly by institutional investors that often hold debt securities until redemption, leaving only a limited number of bonds in a particular issue available for trading among investors. The bottom line for individual investors is that municipal bonds can be difficult to sell, particularly in small amounts, at a fair price. Municipal bond dealers are not eager to purchase small amounts of bonds (i.e., less than $25,000) that are likely to be difficult to resell.

> State tax laws vary regarding the taxation of interest on state and local bonds. You should check on the tax law in effect in the state in which you live before you invest in these bonds. You may find that you must own bonds issued within your state of residence to avoid paying state income taxes on the interest income.

Some municipal bond issues are easier to resell than other issues. Municipal bonds that are a part of large issues from well-known issuers often have an active resale market. Knowledgeable brokers will be able to point you toward bonds that should be actively traded in the event you think you may need to sell your bonds prior to redemption. If you are certain you will hold a municipal bond until maturity, liquidity risk is not a concern and you don't really have to worry about how a bond will trade in the secondary market. Liquidity matters only when you may find yourself wanting to dispose of a bond prior to scheduled redemption.

Tax-Exempt Investment Companies

Many individual investors lack the capital required to acquire a properly diversified portfolio of tax-exempt bonds. Other investors have access to adequate funds but lack the knowledge and confidence to build a portfolio of bond issues. Both groups of investors may find that shares of investment companies holding tax-exempt securities are desirable alternatives to the direct ownership of municipal bonds.

Basics of Tax-Exempt Investment Companies

Tax-exempt investment companies use shareholders' money to purchase municipal bonds for the benefit of the shareholders. Rather than buying buildings and equipment, investment companies buy tax-exempt bonds. When you are the shareholder of an tax-exempt investment company, changes in the value of your investment depend on changes in the value of the investment company's bond portfolio (on a per-share basis). Some tax-exempt investment companies restrict their investments to the municipal bonds of a single state, while other such companies own bonds from many states. Still other tax-exempt investment companies concentrate on owning municipal bonds with long maturities. The returns you achieve as an investment company shareholder depend on the investment success of the company's portfolio managers.

Most investment companies are organized with a corporate structure that permits the issue of additional shares and the redemption of outstanding shares. These companies, called *open-end investment companies* or *mutual funds*, are very popular. *Closed-end investment companies* are organized like most other corporations that have a fixed number of outstanding shares. Shares of closed-end investment companies are traded on organized securities exchanges and in the over-the-counter market. Most closed-end investment companies specialize in bond investments, including tax-exempt municipal bonds.

Tax-exempt unit investment trusts *(UITs, also called unit trusts)* are a close relative of tax-exempt investment companies. Unit trusts hold portfolios of municipal securities that are purchased with funds contributed by investors who purchase ownership shares called *units*. A trust sponsor might put together a $10 million portfolio of municipal bonds financed with 10,000 units sold to investors at $1,000 per unit. Unlike investment companies that are ongoing organizations trading bonds and reinvesting funds received from bond redemptions, unit trusts pass through to unit owners *all* the cash received by the trusts. This includes funds received from bond redemptions as well as interest payments.

And while investment companies actively manage their municipal bond portfolios, unit trusts hold unmanaged portfolios that continually shrink in size as bonds in the portfolios are redeemed. Unit investment trusts charge investors a sales fee but do not ordinarily charge an annual management fee, because no management is required.

Tax Treatment of Investment Company Income

Both closed-end and open-end investment companies are subject to special regulations that require them to pass through the income they earn to their shareholders, who become liable for taxes on the income. Tax-exempt municipal interest that is earned and distributed to shareholders by an investment company is tax-exempt to the shareholders. Long-term capital gains realized from the sale of appreciated municipal bonds are taxed at a maximum rate of 28 percent.

Tax-exempt investment companies and unit trusts are very popular because of strong investor demand for tax-exempt income. Buying shares in a tax-exempt investment company or in a unit trust provides you with partial ownership of a diversified portfolio of tax-exempt municipal bonds. Rather than investing $5,000 or $10,000 in a single bond issue, you can invest the same money in a tax-exempt investment company that may hold a portfolio of hundreds of different tax-exempt bond issues.

Municipal bonds purchased in the secondary market at a discount from face value will result in a taxable gain if you hold the bonds to maturity, even though interest paid by the bond is tax-exempt.

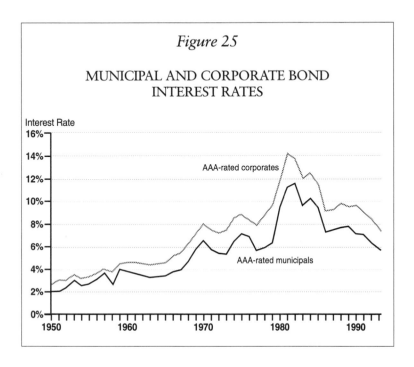

Figure 25

MUNICIPAL AND CORPORATE BOND
INTEREST RATES

Are Tax-Exempt Bonds for You?

Two primary factors determine whether you should own tax-exempt bonds. First, your marginal tax rate must be sufficiently high to allow you to benefit from the tax-free status of municipal bond interest. Tax-exempt bonds have lower pretax yields than either corporate or U.S. treasury bonds. At a time when municipal bonds yield 5 percent, high-grade corporate bonds may offer a taxable return of 7 percent. Choose the tax-free alternative only if taxes on interest income from the 7 percent taxable bond reduce your after-tax yield below 5 percent. Before purchasing a municipal bond, make certain your tax rate is sufficiently high to make the tax-exempt investment the best choice.

The second consideration in deciding whether to purchase municipal bonds is your need for current income. If you have determined that additional current income is important, municipal bonds should be considered as part of your portfolio. If you primarily seek investments with growth potential, fixed-income securities, including tax-exempt bonds, should generally be avoided, and you should concentrate on investments that have capital gains potential, such as common stocks and real estate.

CHAPTER 5

Saving Taxes with Real Estate

Real estate is generally considered to be riskier to own than most financial assets, although adding real estate investments to an existing portfolio of financial assets can reduce overall risk. Your home is a valuable asset, and you should view it as an investment that has the potential to produce both tax savings and capital gains. Direct investments in real estate are generally evaluated using projected cash flows rather than net income. Real estate can produce nominal or negative net income and still prove to be a good investment. Alternative real estate investments, such as partnerships, syndicates, and trusts, are available to investors who choose to have someone else manage their real estate portfolio.

Real estate is big business for builders, speculators, brokers, lenders, institutional investors, individuals, tax collectors, and others. As an investment vehicle, real estate often reigns supreme as families trade up to bigger and fancier homes, financial institutions build huge monoliths to serve as headquarters, and developers open new shopping malls and subdivisions. Many individuals and businesses have earned substantial profits on real estate investments, but not without risk. Real estate can be a volatile investment, one that creates heartache as well as wealth. You may recall the depressing spectacle of former secretary of the treasury and Texas governor John Connally as he witnessed the forced sale of his personal assets following a bankruptcy brought about by real estate investments gone bad.

Real Estate as an Investment

Real estate is a versatile investment that can produce steady monthly income, substantial increases in value, and important tax benefits—*if* things go as planned. Equally important, the investment characteristics of real estate are substantially different from the attributes of most financial assets discussed in earlier chapters. Adding real estate to an existing portfolio of financial assets can result in significant reductions to an investor's overall risk, especially with regard to the effects of inflation.

Factors That Affect the Values of Real Estate Investments

Tangible assets, including real estate, can produce very different investment results compared to those financial assets such as stocks, bonds, and certificates of deposit. Financial assets generally produce the highest real (i.e., inflation-adjusted) returns during periods of steady but moderate economic growth, stable consumer prices, and low or declining interest rates. Real estate investments perform best when economic activity is strong and consumer prices are rising. Real estate, like nearly any other investment, benefits from declining interest rates.

Inflation benefits real estate owners, but not real estate lenders. Real estate values tend to move upward during periods of inflation, often at rates much higher than overall price increases. Land is a limited resource (a fact disputed by all who have driven across Utah and Nevada) that attracts strong investor interest during periods of rapid inflation, as well as when inflation is anticipated. Inflation also benefits the owners of improved real estate. Higher prices for steel, lumber, copper, and construction labor make it more costly to add to the existing stock of homes, office buildings, shopping malls, and factories, an element that in turn drives up the value of the existing stock of improved real estate. In general, inflation is very beneficial for owners of real estate. Inflation has a negative impact on real estate lenders, who are repaid in dollars that have reduced purchasing power.

Interest rates have a major effect on real estate values. Higher interest rates cause real estate purchased on credit to

Selling personal property for more than you paid should be reported as a capital gain and is subject to taxation. Unfortunately, sale of personal property at a loss cannot be used as a deduction in calculating your taxes.

become more expensive to own, thus eliminating many existing and potential investors from the market. The decrease in demand caused by higher interest rates results in declining real estate values. As rising interest rates create a drag on real estate values, fixed-income financial assets become increasingly attractive investment alternatives, thereby further depressing the flow of money into real estate. Both factors can cause the demand for real estate to dry up during periods of unusually high interest rates. Falling interest rates result in less expensive financing that causes real estate values to increase. Lower interest rates reduce mortgage payments and allow more families to qualify for mortgage loans.

Economic activity and population flows play a crucial role in real estate values. Strong economic activity is generally accompanied by business expansion and population inflows that buoy demand for residential, commercial, and industrial properties, thereby benefiting real estate owners with higher rents and increased property values. Real estate values are primarily local phenomena that depend more on local and regional economic activity than on national trends. A strong local economy is likely to result in profitable real estate investments despite weakness in the national economy.

> Real estate values tend to appreciate more during periods of inflation, when the prices of labor, land, and materials are rising. Real estate values are more stable during periods of low or moderate inflation.

Tax Benefits

Real estate investments generally involve substantial amounts of money that cause both buyers and sellers to carefully examine every financial angle. One crucial aspect of a real estate transaction is the effect on the taxes of the parties involved. Real estate owners have, over many years, benefited from a favorable federal tax code. A major financial benefit of real estate is the deductibility of interest on debt that is used to finance residential and commercial real estate purchases. Deductibility of property taxes is another benefit to owners of real estate. Of course, you must actually incur interest charges and pay property taxes before you are entitled to these tax deductions. Tax savings can equal from 15 to 39 percent of the interest and taxes you pay during a given year. Ownership of commercial real estate generates added tax benefits from the depreciation of investment property. The sum of the deductions for interest charges, property taxes, maintenance, and depreciation sometimes offsets all the gross income produced by a property.

Your Home

Your home, which is likely to be the most valuable asset you own, should be considered an important part of your total investment portfolio. Like other investments, a home can produce tax benefits and capital gains or losses. In place of the dividends or interest income you receive from financial assets, ownership of a home will save monthly rental payments you would otherwise make to a landlord. On the downside, investing in a home entails substantial expenses for insurance and maintenance, costs not associated with financial assets.

Tax Benefits of Home Ownership

Home ownership is popular partly because of the associated income tax benefits. Property taxes paid to local authorities and interest charges on loans using a home as collateral can be used as itemized deductions in calculating your federal taxable income. Deductions result in tax savings to the extent that total itemized deductions exceed your allowable standard deduction. Actual tax savings from home ownership depend both on the amount of your deductions and on your marginal tax rate. As discussed in Chapter 2, a higher marginal tax rate causes a given deduction to result in greater tax savings. An additional deduction of $10,000 is worth $2,800 in tax savings for someone in the 28 percent tax bracket, and $3,600 in tax savings for someone who pays a marginal tax rate of 36 percent. Both calculations assume the taxpayer already has sufficient itemized deductions to exceed the allowable standard deduction.

Suppose a childless couple have combined annual salaries and investment income of $62,000. Itemized deductions of $8,500 and exemptions of $4,500 produce $49,000 of tax-

---

Investing in rental real estate often brings headaches as well as tax savings, especially if you decide to manage the property yourself. Receiving midnight calls from tenants about clogged plumbing, a faulty heating unit, or a leaking roof can put you in a bad state of mind.

able income and a federal income tax liability of $8,923 (calculated from Figure 5 in chapter 1). The couple currently pay $850 in monthly rent for a three-bedroom home that is available for purchase. Rent is not deductible for federal income tax purposes and has no effect on the couple's tax liability. The $90,000 purchase price for the home could be financed with a $75,000 loan for twenty years at an annual interest rate of 8 percent. The loan would require 240 monthly payments of $627. Annual property taxes are currently $1,200. Insurance for the home and its contents would cost $600 per year, and maintenance is estimated at $100 monthly. If the couple owned rather than rented this home, they would pay $6,000 in interest charges (8 percent of $75,000) and $1,200 in property taxes during the first year of ownership, thereby increasing their itemized deductions by $7,200, to $15,700. The larger deductions would reduce taxable income from $49,000 to $41,800 (i.e., by the $7,200 increase in deductions), causing the couple's tax liability to fall from $8,923 to $6,907. Thus, the deductibility of interest and property taxes associated with owning rather than renting would allow the couple to save $2,016 in federal income taxes during the first year of ownership.

The tax savings that result from additional deductions equals the amount of the deductions times the taxpayer's marginal income tax rate. In the example just discussed, a higher taxable income that places the couple in the 36 percent marginal tax bracket would cause the $7,200 in additional deductions to save .36 × $7,200, or $2,592, in taxes. This compares with a tax savings of $2,016 at a lower level of taxable income and a 28 percent marginal tax rate. Tax deductions are more valuable to taxpayers with a high marginal tax rate.

Figure 26

THE AFTER-TAX COST OF RENTING VS. OWNING

	Rent	Own
Monthly payment	$ 850	$ 627
Annual payments	10,200	7,524
Annual interest charges (first year)	–	6,000
Annual property taxes	–	1,200
Insurance	120	600
Maintenance	–	1,200
Deductions from taxable income	—	7,200
Tax savings (@ 28 percent rate)	–	2,016
Annual after-tax cost	$10,320	$ 8,508*

*The after-tax cost of owning the home equals the annual loan payments plus property taxes plus insurance plus maintenance less the amount of tax savings.

Gains in Value

Appreciation in the value of your home also receives favorable tax treatment. First, as with other capital assets, increases in value do not affect your taxable income and associated tax liability until the home is sold and the gain realized. You can live in the same home for twenty, thirty, or even fifty years without incurring any income taxes on increases in market value so long as you do not sell the residence.

Even when you do sell, a special section of the tax code allows you to escape taxation, at least temporarily. Any gain from the sale of your primary residence can be deferred indefinitely so long as you purchase another home of equal or greater value to that of the home you sell. Suppose you purchased a home for $65,000 in 1979 that you recently sold for $95,000. If you invest $95,000 or more in another residence within two years of the date the original home is sold (either before or after), tax on the $30,000 gain from the sale of the home is deferred. You can continue your own "parade of homes" and avoid paying taxes on any gains in value so long as you purchase homes that are successively more expensive. The sum of the gains you earn on all these transactions will eventually become taxable when you sell a home you choose not to replace (perhaps you move to an apartment) or when you purchase a less expensive home. If and when you finally sell your home and realize a taxable gain, the applicable tax rate is the same as the rate applied to long-term capital gains. Currently, the maximum federal tax rate on long-term capital gains is 28 percent.

A very special and valuable tax benefit accrues to homeowners who sell a home for a substantial gain but do not wish to reinvest the proceeds in another home of equal value. As a homeowner, you are permitted to exclude up to $125,000 of gains from the sale of a principal residence if

- you are at least fifty-five years old on the date of the sale; *and*

It is nearly always preferable to give appreciated property (i.e., property that has increased in value) rather than cash to charitable organizations. You receive a tax deduction based on the property's market value at the time of the deduction rather than on your cost. This means you get a sizable tax deduction and forever escape taxes on the gains.

Figure 27

WORKSHEET FOR CALCULATING DEFERRED GAINS

Selling price of old home	_____
less: Selling expenses	_____
less: Adjusted basis of old home	_____
Realized gain on sale	_____
Cost of new home	_____
less: Realized gain on sale of old home	_____
Adjusted basis of new home	_____

- you owned and lived in your main home during at least three of the last five years ending on the date the home is sold; *and*
- neither you nor your spouse has excluded a gain on the sale of a residence subsequent to July 26, 1978.

Suppose you purchased your first home for $34,000 in 1960. You later sold this home for $56,000 when you purchased a larger and newer residence for $65,000. The tax on the gain from the sale of your first residence was deferred because you purchased a more expensive home within two years from the date of sale. You are interested in moving to an apartment and have received an offer to purchase your current home for $185,000. If you sell the home, you will have realized gains of $22,000 plus $120,000, or $142,000.

If you qualify for the $125,000 one-time exemption, you will owe taxes on a long-term capital gain of $142,000 less the $125,000 exemption, or $17,000.

Summary of the Tax Benefits of Home Ownership

Home ownership generally results in a reduction in your taxable income that in turn reduces your federal income tax liability. The reduction in taxable income is caused by the large tax deductions that stem from property tax payments and from interest charges on a loan collateralized by your home. It is not unusual to save thousands of dollars annually in federal and state income taxes because of the availability of these two tax deductions.

The downside of the reduction in income taxes associated with home ownership is that you must spend relatively large amounts of money to be able to claim the deductions—you can deduct interest charges and property taxes only after you have paid them. In addition, home ownership involves maintenance expenses and insurance premiums that cannot be deducted. Owning a home entails substantial expenses that are only partially offset by tax savings.

If you choose to make a large down payment when you purchase a home, the reduction in borrowing will result in a smaller monthly payment and reduced interest charges. Less interest in turn means a decrease in the deductions you can claim and a reduction in tax savings. Tax deductions will also decline over time as you pay down the loan balance, thus decreasing annual interest charges. The decline in interest expense and in the associated deduction occurs even though the monthly payment to the lender remains unchanged.

Investment Real Estate

Investment real estate includes rental houses, homes purchased for resale, apartments, undeveloped land, office buildings, warehouses, and so forth. Investment real estate comes in all stripes and prices, although most real estate investments share some commonalities. In particular, the decision to purchase investment real estate generally assumes some appreciation in the value of the property being acquired. The potential for increases in valuation is especially important when only modest rental income will be available to offset the considerable expenses of owning developed property.

The Importance of Cash Flow

Real estate is typically evaluated on the basis of the cash flow it provides, not the income it earns. Income is a paper entry calculated by accountants, while cash flow is money you receive that can be spent or reinvested. A desirable real estate investment may show negative earnings but positive cash flows. On the other hand, you might be willing to invest in a particular piece of real estate that is expected to produce negative cash flows (cash outflows exceeding cash inflows) if you expect the real estate to increase in value. For

Some life insurance companies tack on an extra charge for early withdrawal from annuities. The charge is usually in the form of retroactively crediting your investment with a reduced rate of return. Determine whether the annuity contract contains a provision for an early withdrawal charge (often called a *market value adjustment*) before you purchase the annuity.

example, you may pay a high price for a run-down home that provides only modest rental income because the property is located near an interstate exchange and is likely to be developed in the near future. In this instance, cash flow from rental income is incidental to appreciation in value.

Cash flow in a given year is the sum of all the cash inflows from the asset, typically rental income or revenues from a business operation, less the sum of all the cash outflows. Outflows include maintenance, property taxes, income taxes, insurance, and payments on a loan used to finance the purchase. The amount of cash flow a property generates is important, especially if little or no increase in the value of the property is expected.

Tax Benefits of Investment Real Estate

Most real estate is purchased at least partly because of the tax benefits that accrue to the owner. Ownership of real estate can produce substantial tax savings that transform a moderately good investment into a very good investment. The goal, of course, is to protect large amounts of income—accruing from the real estate itself or from other sources—from taxation. The effectiveness in protecting income from taxation is the bottom line for any tax shelter. Deductions available on most real estate investments include the following:

Interest paid on a loan to finance a real estate investment can be used as a deduction that offsets an equal amount of income. Borrowing $50,000 at 9 percent interest will produce an interest deduction of $4,500 during the first year of the loan. The deduction offsets $4,500 of income that would ordinarily be subject to income taxes. In its effect on taxes the interest deduction for investment real estate is no different from the interest deduction for a home mortgage loan discussed earlier.

Property taxes levied against real estate and paid to state or local authorities are permitted as a deduction from taxable income. The deduction for property taxes you pay on real estate investments is treated in the same manner as property taxes paid on your home (if you itemize deductions). The higher the property taxes you pay, the greater the tax savings you realize.

Insurance premiums for coverage of a real estate investment are a deductible expense from taxable income. Insurance premiums cannot be deducted by homeowners.

Maintenance expenses are fully deductible in calculating the tax liability for a real estate investment. Expenses you incur for repairing rotten wood around the water heater, stopping a leak in the roof, or painting the deck are examples of costs that can be deducted in calculating the income tax liability from ownership of a rental property. Maintenance expenses can be substantial, especially for an older property (or for any property rented to college students), so that being able to deduct these costs is an important benefit of owning investment real estate, one not available to homeowners.

Improvements that prolong the life or increase the value of real estate are treated differently from maintenance. While maintenance expenses can be deducted in the year they are incurred, the costs of improvements must be used to increase the cost basis of the real estate, thereby reducing any gain or increasing any loss when the real estate is eventually sold. For example, adding an additional bathroom and reroofing a rental unit are both improvements that increase the cost basis of the real estate being improved.

Figure 28

EFFECT OF DEPRECIATION ON INCOME AND TAXES

Suppose you purchase rental property that has the following characteristics:

Cost of land	$ 30,000
Cost of building	140,000
Total investment	$ 170,000
Asset life for depreciation	27.5 years
Annual depreciation	$ 5,091*

	Without Depreciation	With Depreciation
Rental income	$ 20,000	$ 20,000
less: Annual depreciation	—	5,091
Taxable income	$ 20,000	$ 14,909
less: Taxes @ 35 percent	7,000	5,218
Net income after taxes	$ 13,000	$ 9,691

* 140,000 ÷ 27.5 years (land is not depreciable)

Depreciation accounts for the decline in the value of an asset, including most real estate, over time. Depreciation decreases the accounting value (the value of the real estate as shown on the financial statements) of real estate and at the same time offsets an equal amount of income from taxation. For example, one year's depreciation of $10,000 decreases the accounting value of a building by $10,000 and offsets $10,000 of income that would otherwise be taxed. Depreciation does not affect the market value of an asset (the price at which the asset could be sold), which can be much different from the value indicated on financial statements. Land, as opposed to buildings and equipment, cannot be depreciated.

Investors generally derive maximum tax benefits by depreciating real estate as quickly as possible. Rapid depreciation offsets income and saves taxes sooner. It is to your advantage to save $3,000 in taxes this year as opposed to saving $600 per year over the next five years. To standardize the depreciation of like assets, the Internal Revenue Service has established estimated lives for all types of assets, including real estate. A vehicle purchased for business use must be depreciated over five years, for example, and a refrigerator or stove in a rental property must be depreciated over seven years. You are not permitted to depreciate property purchased for personal use. For example, you cannot depreciate your own home or the appliances it contains. Residential rental property currently must be depreciated over twenty-seven and a half years, a relatively long period compared to the depreciation of other assets that have considerably shorter life spans.

Real Estate Investment Evaluation

Suppose you purchase a piece of rental property for the anticipated rental income, tax savings, and appreciation in the property's value. You pay $30,000 down on the $180,000 purchase price and borrow the remaining $150,000 with a twenty-five–year loan at 8 percent interest. The loan stipulates end-of-year payments of $14,059 to cover each year's annual interest charge and a portion of the outstanding principal. Depreciation will be calculated on a straight-line basis, meaning that the annual depreciation charge will remain the same throughout the property's twenty-seven-and-a-half year life. The $180,000 purchase price is allocated $25,000 to land and $155,000 to the building. Only the latter can be depreciated. Annual depreciation will equal $155,000 ÷ 27.5 years, or $5,636 each year the property is owned. Annual property taxes will be $2,600 in the first year of ownership and will increase by 5 percent annually thereafter. Insurance on the property is expected to cost $2,100 per year. First-year maintenance is estimated at $3,600, an amount that should increase by 8 percent annually. On the revenue side you expect gross rental income of $25,000 in the first year, with anticipated increases of 6 percent each year thereafter. An expected 5 percent vacancy rate will cause net rental income (the income you will actually receive) to average 95 percent of gross rental income (the amount you would receive if the property were fully rented).

The property is in an excellent location and has a good potential for long-term appreciation. You intend to sell the real estate at the end of three years and use the proceeds to pay off the balance of the twenty-five–year loan. Based on the estimated rental income at that time, you expect to be able to sell the property for $200,000. The applicable tax rate on capital gains is 28 percent.

Several techniques can be used to evaluate the return an asset provides. One method is to estimate the annual after-

---

The maximum 28 percent rate applies to long-term capital gains but not short-term capital gains. Short-term capital gains are treated as ordinary income for tax purposes. You must hold a capital asset (stock, bonds, real estate, etc.) for *more than one year* to have a gain or loss qualify as long-term.

Figure 29

ANNUAL TAXES AND NET INCOME
FOR A RENTAL PROPERTY

	First Year	Second Year	Third Year
Gross rental income	$25,000	$26,500	$28,090
less: Expected vacancies (5 percent)	– 1,250	– 1,325	– 1,404
Net rental income	$23,750	$25,175	$26,686
less: Deductible cash expenses			
Insurance	– $ 2,100	– $ 2,100	– $ 2,100
Maintenance	– 3,600	– 3,888	– 4,199
Property taxes	– 2,600	– 2,730	– 2,866
Interest	– 12,000	– 11,835	– 11,657
Total deductible cash expenses	$20,300	$20,553	$20,822
plus: Depreciation	+ 5,636	+ 5,636	+ 5,636
Total pretax expenses	$25,936	$26,189	$26,458
Taxable income	($ 2,186)	($ 1,014)	$ 228
Income taxes (@ 36 percent)	(787)	(365)	82
Net income after taxes	($ 1,399)	($ 649)	$ 146

tax income that will be earned. A superior technique is to compare the cash outflow associated with the purchase with the estimated net cash inflows you expect to receive during the period of ownership. Cash inflows should include net proceeds received from the sale of the property as well as rental income earned during the time the property is owned.

Annual Taxes and Net Income. The first step in evaluating the rental property is to calculate the pretax income you can expect to earn during each of the three years of ownership. Pretax, or taxable, income is calculated by subtracting deductible expenses (maintenance, property taxes, insurance, interest expense, and depreciation) from forecasted net rental income. Taxable income is then used as a basis to calculate each year's taxes and net income. Large expenses relative to rental income may cause the project to produce accounting losses (negative pretax and after-tax income) that result in net tax savings.

Estimated revenues and expenses from Figure 29 indicate that ownership of the rental property will produce accounting losses during each of the first two years and only a small profit during the third year. Projected losses during each of the first two years will result in tax savings (negative taxes) if the losses can be used to offset other sources of income. The calculations so far exclude consideration of the capital gain that is anticipated when the property is sold. The treatment and effect of the expected capital gain will be discussed shortly.

Annual Cash Flows. The rental property's cash flows are different from the net income just calculated. First, when calculating net income, depreciation is a deduction that reduces both taxable income and income taxes. The reduction in income taxes, which is a cash expense, improves the property's cash flow. Depreciation itself, however, is a noncash expense (i.e., it doesn't require a cash outlay) that reduces taxable income but does not reduce cash flow.

The entire amount of each year's loan payment ($14,059) is used in calculating net cash flow. Only the interest portion of the loan payments is used in calculating net income because only interest expense is deductible in calcu-

---

Figure 30

ANNUAL CASH FLOWS FROM A RENTAL PROPERTY

	First Year	Second Year	Third Year
Net rental income	$23,750	$25,175	$26,686
less: Cash expenses			
Insurance	− $ 2,100	− $ 2,100	− $ 2,100
Maintenance	− 3,600	− 3,888	− 4,199
Property taxes	− 2,600	− 2,730	− 2,866
Income taxes	− (787)	− (365)	− 82
Payment on loan	− 14,059	− 14,059	− 14,059
Total cash expenses	$21,572	$22,412	$23,306
Net cash flow	$ 2,178	$ 2,763	$ 3,380

---

lating taxable income. The difference between a loan payment and the applicable interest expense can be large, especially for short-term loans or in the final years of a long-term loan. The loan payment rather than interest expense is used in Figure 30 to calculate the real estate investment's cash flow.

Cash Flow from the Sale of the Property. Net cash flows from rental income cease after three years, when you sell the property. The final cash flow from the investment, the amount of cash you net from the sale, depends on a variety of factors, including the sale price, expenses you incur in the sale (e.g., repairs, commission to a realtor), and income taxes you may be required to pay on a realized gain in the

---

Figure 31

NET CASH FLOW FROM
THE SALE OF A RENTAL PROPERTY

Proceeds from Sale

Sale price	$200,000
less: Commission	− 12,000
Net proceeds from sale	$188,000

Taxable Basis

Purchase price	$180,000
less: Accumulated depreciation	− 16,908
Adjusted cost or basis	$163,092

Tax from Sale

Net proceeds from sale	$188,000
less: Adjusted basis	− 163,092
Taxable proceeds (capital gain)	$ 24,908
Income tax (@ 28 percent)	$ 6,974

Cash Flow from Sale

Net proceeds from sale	$188,000
less: Tax on gain	− 6,974
less: Payoff on loan*	− 143,315
Net cash from sale	$ 37,711

* Original amount borrowed less reduction in principal from three years of loan payments (sum of payments less three years of interest).

---

value of the property. Figure 31 illustrates the method of calculating the cash flow from the sale.

Cash flow information from Figures 30 and 31 allows you to determine the after-tax rate of return you can expect from the purchase and ownership of the rental property. The exact after-tax return is the discount rate *(i)* that equates the present value of the four cash inflows with your initial net outlay of $30,000. This is shown as

$$\$30,000 \ = \ \frac{\$2,178}{(1+i)^1} + \frac{\$2,763}{(1+i)^2} + \frac{\$3,380}{(1+i)^3} + \frac{\$37,711}{(1+i)^3}$$

This formula can be solved with most financial calculators or by simply estimating a rate and working out the numbers to determine if your estimate is too high or too low—a process that leads to a second attempt with a more accurate estimate and that is then repeated until the two sides of the equation are equal. A reasonable estimate of the annual return on your $30,000 investment can be calculated using the following method:

1. Determine the amount by which total cash inflows exceed the outlay. For this particular investment the excess cash flow is equal to the sum of the four cash inflows ($46,032) less your cash outlay ($30,000), or $16,032.
2. Divide the excess cash flow ($16,032) by the number of years you hold the investment (three) to determine the average annual excess cash flow produced by the investment. The rental property produces an average surplus cash flow of $16,032 ÷ 3, or $5,344 during each year of

Cash, securities, or other property you inherit from an estate is not considered taxable income to you, although you are likely to have to pay inheritance taxes. Large estates left to other than a surviving spouse are taxed by the federal government.

ownership. The excess cash flow includes the cash profit from selling the property as well as the cash rent received each year the property was owned.

3. Determine the approximate annual return by dividing the average annual cash flow by your initial cash outlay. The after-tax return is calculated as $5,344 ÷ $30,000, or 17.8 percent. This compares with an actual annual return of 16.3 percent, using the formula presented above.

CHAPTER 6

Saving Taxes with Insurance

Certain products sold by life insurance companies can decrease your current income taxes. Like most tax shelters, insurance products offer greater tax benefits to high-income individuals who pay high marginal tax rates. The accumulation of savings within life insurance policies and annuities escapes taxation until funds are paid out by the insurance company to the investor. Annuities are generally purchased to supplement other sources of retirement income such as Social Security and employer-sponsored pension plans. Annuities can be purchased by making monthly or annual payments during your working lifetime or by making a single, large payment.

Many large life insurance companies have been transformed into financial conglomerates that offer a wide range of financial services and products. Today's multifaceted companies contrast sharply with the notion held by many individuals that life insurance companies offer life insurance and nothing else. To remain competitive with brokerage companies and large money centers and regional banks, life insurers have developed new products and modified existing insurance contracts to attract new customers. The pressure for more competitive products was especially acute during the 1980s, when high interest rates caused many financial planners and consumers to shun the life insurers' most profitable product, cash value life insurance.

A major factor in the desirability of life insurance products as investments concerns the favorable tax treatment these products receive. In general, savings that accumulate from premiums paid into a life insurance policy or an annuity remain free of income taxes until the funds are eventually withdrawn, and even then only a portion of the payouts received is subject to taxation.

Life Insurance Products

The primary product sold by life insurance companies provides death benefits to individuals or organizations upon the death of the insured. The most basic life insurance product requires increasing annual premiums for as long as the insured lives. Premium payments cease at the death of the insured, when the face value of the policy is paid to the named beneficiaries or to the estate of the insured. A second type of life insurance requires fixed annual premiums that last from ten years to a lifetime, depending on the particular type of policy chosen.

Term Insurance

Term insurance is often described as "pure insurance" because at the insured's death it pays the face value of the policy to one or more beneficiaries named by the insured. No other benefits accrue to the insured or any other party. A term insurance policy is in force for a limited time, or "term," after which the policy must be renewed, generally at an increased premium. Premiums increase as you grow older because the chance of your dying in a given year increases, thus making it more likely that the insurance company will have to pay the face value of your policy.

Because these policies pay only at the death of the insured, premium payments for term life insurance are relatively low. No savings build up in a term insurance policy, so that no funds are returned to you as the policyholder if you stop paying premiums and cancel the policy. You can pay premiums on a term insurance policy for twenty years, thirty years, or longer, without receiving any financial benefits. On the other hand, you have purchased the peace of mind of knowing your dependents will receive financial support in the event of your death.

When evaluating life insurance as a tax-saving investment keep in mind that this product requires that you pay for life insurance that you may or may not need. If you don't require life insurance coverage, your after-tax returns are likely to be improved by choosing another type of investment.

There is really only one income tax benefit to term life insurance. Suppose you purchase a $50,000 face value policy and assign your spouse as beneficiary. After making three annual premium payments of $420, $440, and $470, you suffer a fatal heart attack. The $50,000 that is paid by the insurance company to your spouse is *free* of any income taxes even though you paid only $1,330 in total premiums on the policy. Proceeds of a life insurance policy paid to a beneficiary are not considered taxable income but may be subject to estate or inheritance taxes depending on the size of the estate, the relationship of the beneficiary, and the state of residence of the policyholder and the beneficiary.

Cash Value Insurance

Cash value life insurance includes both savings and the death benefit of term insurance. If you decide to cancel a cash value life insurance policy on which you have been paying premiums for more than two or three years, you can expect to receive a cash settlement for savings that have accumulated in the policy. The longer you have been paying premiums, the larger the cash payment you will receive from the insurance company.

Cash value accumulates in a life insurance policy only because the premiums you pay exceed the cost of your in-

For many years life insurance companies were considered to have a "rock-solid" credit quality. High credit quality among insurers can no longer be assumed, and you should be certain to carefully examine an insurance company's financial status before purchasing an annuity or life insurance policy.

surance. Whereas term insurance requires only that you pay the cost of the death benefit, cash value insurance requires that you pay for the death benefit *plus* an additional amount that causes savings to accumulate within the policy. While you might pay an annual premium of $450 at age thirty for $100,000 of term insurance, a policy that accumulates a cash value might involve an annual premium of $1,500 or even $2,000.

Insurance companies offer several types of cash value life insurance policies. Differences among the policies stem primarily from the number of years a policyholder agrees to pay premiums. For a given amount of life insurance coverage, more scheduled premiums mean lower premiums and a slower buildup of savings. On the other hand, a life insurance policy that remains in force for a lifetime but requires only ten annual premiums will have high premiums that rapidly build cash values. Cash buildup within the policy is used to take care of the insurance cost in the years following the scheduled end of premiums. Following is a description of some of the more popular types of cash value life insurance policies.

Straight Life Insurance. Straight life insurance (also called *whole life)* requires that you pay fixed annual premiums over your entire lifetime. In the early years of the policy, the premium is at a level that is greater than the cost of providing insurance. (This allows the policy to build cash value.) As you grow older and the cost of insurance increases, the accumulated cash value supplements premium payments that are too low to cover the cost of insurance. A special type of whole life insurance, called *modified whole life,* stipulates reduced premiums during the early years the policy is in force. At a specified point—say, five years after the policy is issued—the premium is raised beyond the premium that would be charged for a regular straight life policy. Straight life insurance builds savings more slowly than other types of cash value insurance.

Limited-Payment Life Insurance. Limited-payment life insurance requires that you pay premiums for a stipulated number of years. High premiums for these policies cause cash values to accumulate rapidly until they are sufficient to cover the cost of insurance after scheduled premiums cease. Suppose at age twenty-five you purchase a $50,000 life insurance policy that stipulates twenty equal annual premiums (called *twenty-pay life*). When you reach age forty-five, the policy will be fully paid and no further premiums will be necessary, even though your life insurance coverage continues and the cash value in the policy continues to build, although at a reduced rate compared to the buildup when you were paying premiums. Other popular limited-payment policies include thirty-pay life and paid-up at sixty-five.

Single-Premium Life Insurance. A single-premium life insurance policy requires you pay only a single large premium to buy life insurance that will remain in force for your entire life. The premium you pay is so much greater than the cost of insuring you in the first year of the policy that the re-

Expenses charged to policyholders vary substantially among different insurance companies. Always be certain to aggressively shop among several life insurance companies before you commit to buying a policy. If you have difficulty comparing policies, consult an independent reference, such as *Consumer Reports,* that periodically evaluates the policies of different companies.

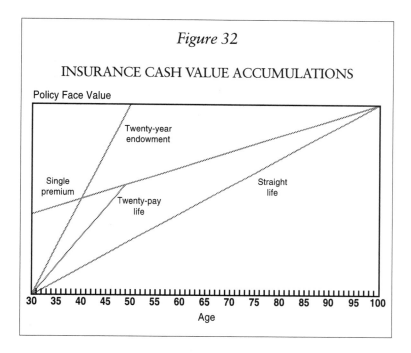

Figure 32

INSURANCE CASH VALUE ACCUMULATIONS

Policy Face Value

Twenty-year endowment

Single premium

Twenty-pay life

Straight life

Age

30 35 40 45 50 55 60 65 70 75 80 85 90 95 100

maining cash value covers the cost of your death benefits in each subsequent year *and still increases in size.* The single-premium policy is marketed by insurance companies primarily as a tax-advantaged investment. The tax advantage comes from the fact that the policy's increases in cash value avoid current taxation. Special tax rules require the owner of a single-premium policy to pay taxes on withdrawals and loans from policy earnings. As with IRAs, withdrawals or loans prior to age fifty-nine and a half are subject to a 10 percent penalty.

Universal Life Insurance. This unique type of life insurance was introduced in the late 1970s to compete with investment alternatives such as bonds and certificates of deposit that offered high returns in an economic environment of high interest rates. Savings in universal life policies are invested in short-term debt securities that earn market rates of return. Cash values accumulate to the extent that premiums exceed the cost of death benefits and according to the returns that cash values earn. Universal life insurance permits a policyholder to alter both the premium payments and the death benefits. A policyholder is also permitted to borrow or withdraw—without paying taxes—any portion of the policy's cash value that does not exceed the total of premiums that have been paid.

Variable-Universal Life Insurance. This type of life insurance offers flexibility with respect to the premium you pay, the face value of the policy, and the assets in which your cash values are invested. Rather than having the policy's cash value invested only in fixed-income securities (as is the case with regular universal life insurance), variable-universal life insurance allows you to choose from among stock, bond, and money market mutual funds. Cash values invested in mutual funds are maintained by a trustee who is independent of the insurance company that sold the product. This independence means that the insurance company or creditors of the insurance company are unable to obtain access to the funds, a provision that can be very beneficial to

Cash values in life insurance policies build up slowly during the initial years. Life insurance companies typically front-load their fees so that it would not be unusual to get little or nothing back if you cancel a policy after the second or third year.

a policyholder in the event the insurance company encounters financial difficulties.

Endowment. An endowment is a special type of life insurance policy that pays the face value to your beneficiaries at your death (as is the case with other life insurance policies) or pays *you* the face value at the end of a specified period. For example, a $50,000, twenty-year endowment policy pays $50,000 to you if you remain alive at the end of twenty years or it pays $50,000 to your designated beneficiary if you die before twenty years elapse. Thus, with an endowment policy the full face value is paid by a specified date whether you die or remain alive.

Cash values build rapidly in endowment policies because of the high premiums these policies require. The majority of the premium payments go to savings so that the cash value can build to the face value by the scheduled termination date of the policy. Taxation of cash buildups is deferred until funds are withdrawn from the policy or until the face amount is paid. Tax is owed on the amount by which the payment to a policyholder exceeds the sum of the premiums that have been paid. Payment of the face value to a beneficiary in the event of the death of the insured does not result in any income taxes, although the payment may result in estate taxes or inheritance taxes.

Annuities

An annuity promises to pay a specific sum periodically for a specified number of years. For example, you may purchase an annuity that promises to pay $1,500 monthly for thirty years. Or perhaps you are interested in arranging for retirement income to begin in fifteen years, when you plan to quit work. Annuities are an investment product sold by life insurance companies, brokerage firms, mutual funds, banks, and financial planners. The cost of an annuity varies, depending on your age, your sex, the number of lives covered, the date when payments are to begin, and the method used to distribute benefits.

Immediate and Deferred Annuities

Insurance companies offer annuities that make annual payments beginning immediately or at a specified date in the future. If you are near retirement, you may want to purchase an *immediate annuity*, which begins making monthly payments immediately. Purchasing an immediate annuity requires that you pay the full cost of the annuity in a single lump sum. For example, a $100,000 payment may purchase a monthly annuity of $1,200 for long as you live. A larger payment on your part will purchase an annuity that pays a larger monthly income. An immediate annuity is appropriate for an individual who has accumulated a large pool of funds that he or she wishes to convert into a lifetime income.

Alternatively, insurance companies sell *deferred annuities,* with annual payments that begin on a specified date in

Term life insurance does not offer any tax benefits but it does offer low premiums compared to those of cash value life insurance, especially when purchased at a young age. Most young parents can afford the proper amount of life insurance coverage by purchasing term insurance only.

the future. Perhaps you wish to receive monthly payments of $1,000 beginning in thirty years, when you expect to retire at age sixty. A deferred annuity can be purchased by making a lump-sum payment (e.g., at age thirty you pay $40,000 to the insurance company, which, in turn, promises to provide you with monthly payments of $1,000 that begin when you reach age sixty). A deferred annuity can also be purchased by making a series of monthly or annual payments. Rather than part with a single large amount, you may choose to make annual payments of $2,000 from age thirty to age sixty, at which time the insurance company will begin paying you.

Variable Annuities

Variable annuities offer the advantages of investing in mutual funds (potentially high returns, diversification, protection from inflation, etc.) along with the added advantage of deferring taxes on investment income. Variable annuities make periodic payments that vary in size depending on the investment performance of the assets in which the funds are invested. Typically, payments to a variable annuity are invested in common stocks or in a combination of common stocks and bonds. The performance of the stock and bond markets determines the return that is earned by the annu-

The 1986 Tax Reform Act greatly complicated the tax implications of investing in cash value life insurance. If you are contemplating a large investment in life insurance, make certain to determine the tax implications before, rather than after, committing your funds.

ity's invested funds. The higher the return that is earned, the more rapidly an annuitant's pool of savings grows and the greater the size of the payments that will eventually be received. High returns increase the size of payments for both immediate and deferred variable annuities. Financial experts advise individuals who are considering the purchase of a variable annuity to check the investment history over a period of ten to twenty years. This information is available in the A. M. Best reference books that are in many libraries.

Variable annuities also offer the possibility of reduced payments caused by a decline in the value of the investments in which an annuitant's contributions have been invested. If you purchase an immediate or deferred annuity linked to stock market performance, a major market decline could cause you to receive payments that are considerably smaller than you expected when you purchased the annuity. Variable annuities involve high annual fees and steep commissions that can exceed 100 percent of first-year premiums.

Tax Aspects of Annuities

An annuity generally shields investment income from taxation until funds are paid to the annuitant. Thus, annuities provide tax deferral rather than tax savings. The downside is that withdrawals from annuities prior to age fifty-nine

---

The insurance company that offers the lowest prices on term policies may be less competitive on cash value policies or on annuities. It is important to shop among companies for the specific type of insurance product you plan to purchase.

Annuities and life insurance are long-term financial commitments that deserve a careful investigation of an insurer's financial health. For greatest safety, select an insurance company with an A+ rating from A. M. Best.

and a half are treated in the same manner as early withdrawals from an individual retirement account. That is, except in unusual circumstances, early withdrawals are subject to a 10 percent penalty. Another important consideration is that the Internal Revenue Service treats withdrawals as fully taxable until an annuitant's balance falls to the total amount he or she has paid into the annuity.

Suppose you have paid $500 monthly into an annuity for a period of twenty-five years and your annual investment return has averaged 7 percent. Following the last of your 300 payments you will have paid a total of $150,000 (300 payments of $500 each) into a fund that will amount to $405,036. If you subsequently begin receiving $4,000 of monthly income from the annuity, *all* of the payments will be taxable until your account balance falls to $150,000, the total amount you paid into the annuity. Subsequent withdrawals will not be taxable.

CHAPTER 7

Deferring Taxes with Retirement Accounts

Tax-sheltered retirement accounts allow you to invest and earn returns on pretax rather than posttax dollars. Taxes must be paid eventually, but probably at rates that are lower after retirement compared to the rates you pay during your working years. Several tax-sheltered retirement alternatives are available, including Individual Retirement Accounts (IRAs), Keogh plans, 401(k) and 403(b) plans, profit sharing, and other pension plans. Each alternative has different restrictions with regard to who qualifies, the amount and timing of contributions, and the timing and procedures for withdrawals. Contributions to an appropriate tax-sheltered plan can provide thousands of additional dollars for your retirement years.

This chapter was written by W. Kent Moore. Dr. Moore is Professor of Management and Associate Dean in the College of Business Administration at Valdosta State University. Professor Moore received his Ph.D at the University of Texas at Austin. He is an Elvis fan.

Several factors should be considered when you establish a financial plan for retirement. It is best to begin at a young age so that contributions can be made over a long period of time. This allows your plan to accumulate more earnings on the contributions, and it puts less pressure on you to make large contributions every year. You should make certain you diversify the assets you own to guard against major losses of principal. You should choose assets that offer the likelihood of providing a favorable return, and you should try to shelter the return from current taxation in order to accumulate a greater amount of assets. Tax-sheltered retirement savings plans, especially if started early in your career, provide an excellent method for saving taxes during your working years.

Advantages of Tax-Sheltered Retirement Plans

Tax-sheltered retirement plans are approved by the government as a means of allowing people to invest pretax dollars and defer payment of federal income taxes until later in life, usually after retirement. State and local income taxes are also often deferred. Employer contributions to tax-sheltered pension plans are not subject to Social Security payroll taxes, but

Don't assume you will be paying a lower tax rate on your income at retirement than you are paying currently. Even though you may have a reduced level of income at retirement, you may find that the income will be taxed at a higher rate. There is no way to forecast the income tax rates that will be in effect ten, twenty, or even more years down the road.

employee contributions are treated as Social Security wages for FICA tax purposes. Tax-sheltered plans make it possible for investors to attain a substantially larger cash buildup during their earning years and thus to have a much larger amount of money available during their retirement years.

The tax deferral of qualified retirement plans works in a manner similar to that of the cash buildups in life insurance and annuity contracts, discussed in the previous chapter. Suppose that your marginal federal income tax rate is 28 percent. If you decide to save $100 per month for retirement, you can put $100 of your take-home pay (after-tax dollars) into a savings account. Alternatively, you can put $100 of before-tax dollars in a qualified tax-sheltered plan. The second alternative reduces your take-home pay by only $72 because your current tax liability declines by $28. Contributions to the plan cost even less if state and local taxes are also deferred. Keep in mind that income taxes are not waived, but only deferred until retirement, when your marginal tax rate might be lower. As pointed out later in this chapter, however, *even if your marginal tax rate remains the same during your retirement years as in your earning years,* a tax-sheltered plan allows you to have more money during retirement.

Tax-deferred retirement plans offer the added advantage of providing you with more investment flexibility. Whereas you generally need to consider the tax consequences of liquidating nonsheltered investments, tax-sheltered plans allow you to move from one investment to another whenever you wish, because there are no capital gains taxes to pay. Keep in mind that you are likely to incur a fee when you trade one investment asset for another.

Employer Pension Plans

Until about thirty years ago, retirements were funded primarily by Social Security, employer pension plans, and individual savings or investments. Employer pension plans fall into two broad categories—defined-contribution plans and defined-benefit plans.

A *defined-contribution plan* specifies the amount an employer will contribute but does not promise a specific benefit amount to the employee. A plan participant who retires or otherwise becomes eligible for benefits is entitled to the total amount in his or her account, including earnings on contributions that have been made by the employer. The most common defined-contribution plan is a money-purchase pension plan, in which an employer regularly sets aside money (usually a percentage of the employee's wages) for an employee's retirement. Sometimes employees contribute to the plan as well. Contributions and earnings on these plans typically accumulate tax-free until they are withdrawn. The amount of money available at retirement depends both on the amount that is contributed and on the success of investments in the retirement fund.

A *defined-benefit plan* does not require an employer to make a specific contribution each year. Rather, the plan specifies the benefits that are promised at retirement, based upon an employee's income and years of employment.

Employer-sponsored plans in the United States are about equally divided between the two categories, but many companies are shifting to defined-contribution plans. Defined-contribution plans create more uncertainty for employees concerning the amount of benefits they will receive, but these plans are also easier to transfer from one account to another (i.e., they have more portability).

Individual Retirement Accounts

Individual Retirement Accounts (IRAs) were established in 1974 for the purpose of allowing employees to supplement retirement funds provided by Social Security and/or employer pension plans.

Like some other retirement savings plans, an IRA provides numerous investment possibilities for contributed funds. Alternatives include bonds, stocks, mutual funds, money market accounts, certificates of deposit, treasury bills, government securities and agency notes, insurance annuities, and American Eagle coins. Tangible personal property and collectibles such as works of art, stamps, and antiques are not permissible investments.

Types of IRAs

1. *Contributory IRAs,* also called *regular* or *individual IRAs,* are opened by employed individuals who want to set aside part of their annual compensation for retire-

If you have an IRA, be certain the financial institution handling it makes the *required* distributions in a timely manner. Failure to receive the required distributions subjects you to paying a substantial penalty.

ment. This is the most common type of Individual Retirement Account.

2. *Spousal IRAs* enable a working spouse to contribute to an IRA established for his or her spouse. Spousal IRA contributions require that each spouse open a separate account because the law does not allow IRA accounts to be jointly owned.

3. *Third-party-sponsored IRAs* are established by employers, unions, or employee associations for the purpose of making contributions on behalf of employees.

4. A *Simplified Employee Pension Plan (SEP)* is established to allow an employer to provide retirement benefits for employees by making contributions to their IRAs. A SEP has a much higher contribution limit than a third-party sponsored IRA. Employers, however, must establish a written allocation formula for determining contributions and must treat all employees equally, a factor that tends to keep contributions well below the maximum.

5. A *rollover contribution* is a distribution from an IRA or an employer's qualified plan to a participant, who subsequently reinvests all or part of the distribution in another IRA. Several types of rollovers are permitted, but various timing and procedural restrictions apply.

Participants in contributory, spousal, and third-party sponsored IRAs must be receiving compensation during the year IRA contributions are made. IRA law makes a distinction between income and compensation. Figure 33 provides examples of the types of income that are included and excluded as compensation. Although contributions must be *based* on compensation, a participant's actual contributions can come from any source.

Figure 33

TYPES OF INCOME

Income Defined as Compensation	Income Not Defined as Compensation
Salaries and wages	Investment earnings and rent
Professional fees	Interest from deposit accounts
Sales commissions	Investments without a working
Income based on a	interest (silent partnership)
percentage of profits	Social Security and early
Bonuses and tips	retirement income
Self-employment income	Unemployment compensation
Alimony	Disability pay

Regulations Concerning IRA Contributions

Contributions to IRAs are regulated with regard to the amount that may be contributed, the amount that may be taken as a deduction from taxable income, and the timing of the contributions. The maximum allowable amounts for each of the five types of IRA contributions and for other types of contributions that will be discussed later are shown in Figure 34. Tax reform passed in 1986 restricted annual deductible contributions even further. Single workers with an adjusted gross income (AGI) below $25,000 and married workers with an AGI below $40,000 can still contribute the full $2,000. For those with AGIs above these amounts, the allowable deductible contribution is reduced $1.00 for each $5.00 increase in income until the allowable deductible contribution is entirely phased out, at $35,000 for single workers and $50,000 for married workers.

Figure 34

MAXIMUM ALLOWABLE CONTRIBUTIONS FOR RETIREMENT PLANS

Type of Account	Maximum Allowable Amount
Contributory IRA	$2,000 or 100 percent of compensation, whichever is less. Less for "higher income" individuals (see text).
Spousal IRA	$2,250 or 100 percent of compensation, whichever is less. No more than $2,000 may be contributed to the account of either spouse. Less for "higher income" individuals (see text).
Third-party-sponsored IRA	Same as contributory or spousal limits, whichever is applicable.
Regular SEP IRA	$30,000 or 15 percent of compensation, whichever is less. Also, an employee may contribute an extra $2,000 each year.
Rollover IRA	No limitation.
401(k) plan and salary deferral SEP IRA	$8,994 in 1993, reindexed annually, for employee pretax contributions. Lesser of $30,000 or 25 percent of compensation for combined employer and employee contributions.
403(b) plan	$9,500 to $12,500 for employee pretax contributions. Lesser of $30,000 or 20 percent of compensation for combined employer and employee contributions.
Keogh plan (money-purchase)	Lesser of $30,000 or 20 percent of compensation. Percentage must be the same each year.
Keogh plan (profit-sharing)	Lesser of $30,000 or 13.043 percent of compensation. Percentage can be changed each year.

Nondeductible IRA contributions require the use of after-tax dollars and, as a result, have not been very popular. Keep in mind, however, that the *earnings* from nondeductible contributions are tax deferred. Although nondeductible IRAs are not attractive compared to other retirement plans discussed in this chapter, they are still generally preferable to putting money into investments when earnings are not tax deferred.

The timing of contributions is based upon the taxable year, which is the twelve-month period that an individual uses as the basis for calculating federal income taxes. The taxable year for most taxpayers is the same as the calendar year. Contributions to an IRA are considered to be part of a taxable year if they are made by April 15 of the *following* year. So, for example, contributions made anytime from January 1 of one year through April 15 of the following year can be regarded as contributions in the first year. Contributions you make during the leeway period from January 1 to April 15 of the following year must specify to which year the contributions will be applied. This flexibility allows you to contribute more than $2,000 in a taxable year. For

One of the main reasons to choose investments that defer taxes is your belief that you will be in a lower tax bracket when taxable income is finally paid. If you end up in a significantly higher tax bracket, you may find that you would have been better off to have paid the taxes in an earlier year. Although you would think you should be in a lower tax bracket after retirement, you may find that the government has raised tax rates or you may have underestimated the amount of retirement income to be received.

example, suppose you contribute $3,000 to a contributory IRA in a single year ($1,000 contributions on April 1, July 1, and October 1). You have not violated the $2,000 limit for the year, because you can apply the $1,000 contributed on April 1 to the previous year (unless you have already contributed the maximum $2,000 in that year).

IRA Distributions

Distributions are withdrawals from retirement plans. An IRA participant between the ages of fifty-nine and a half and seventy and a half is allowed to take distributions without penalty at any time and for any amount up to the value of the account. Participants under age fifty-nine and a half are penalized for making withdrawals, except in the few cases discussed below. A participant is required to begin taking distributions at age seventy and a half. Financial institutions where IRA funds are invested should inform participants with regard to which distributions can be taken without adverse tax consequences and which distributions will be penalized. Both the institution and the participant are required to report withdrawals to the IRS. Institutions must obtain and report the reason for a withdrawal.

Methods of Receiving Distributions

IRA participants can choose from three methods of distribution. First, they may withdraw the entire balance in the IRA as a single lump-sum distribution. To partially alleviate the tax burden, individuals receiving a lump sum may use income averaging over a five-year period, or if they were born before 1936, over a ten-year period. Second, they may purchase a single life annuity or a joint life and last survivor annuity for the participant, covering the participant and spouse. Third, they may begin to receive distributions over a predetermined period of time, called a *period certain*, according to a payout schedule based on life expectancies.

Once you select a distribution method at the beginning of the second year of withdrawals, you must stick with it. If you die after age seventy and a half, the remainder of your IRA must be paid to your heirs at least as fast as occured with the distribution method used before your death. If you die before age seventy and a half, the distribution can be accomplished (1) by December 31 of the fifth year after death or (2) in annual amounts over the life expectancy of the heir.

Early Distributions

IRA distributions generally cannot be made without penalty before age fifty-nine and a half, but there are exceptions. A participant may name a beneficiary to receive IRA funds upon the participant's death. This transfer can take place without penalty. IRA beneficiaries, except for surviving spouses, must receive lump-sum or periodic payment distributions within five years of the participant's death. Distributions can be taken from an IRA without penalty if a participant becomes disabled. Also, under a divorce decree part or all of the proceeds of an IRA may be transferred

> Tax deferrals are valuable, but not as valuable as actually avoiding (legally, of course) taxes. Deferred taxes must eventually be paid, while legal tax avoidance reduces the taxes you must pay. It's better not to pay at all than to pay later.

without penalty to an IRA in the name of a former spouse. You may withdraw funds from an IRA before age fifty-nine and a half without paying a penalty *if* you take the money in equal periodic payments designed to last the rest of your life. You must take the payments for at least five years *and* until you are at least fifty-nine and a half. After that, the payout rate can be changed. Finally, distributions can be used to make rollover contributions or to remedy excess contributions.

Summary of IRAs

The advantages of IRAs far outweigh the disadvantages, especially when contributions are deductible from taxable income. Earnings for either deductible or nondeductible IRAs grow faster than ordinary savings accounts, because IRA earnings are tax deferred, allowing all earnings to be reinvested. Even when withdrawals are made, the remaining funds continue to grow as tax-deferred assets. For deductible IRAs, contributions are subtracted from income for federal income tax purposes. The two major disadvantages to IRAs are (1) the small allowable annual contribution and (2) the numerous regulations that must be carefully followed to avoid penalties.

401(k) and 403(b) Plans

These tax-deferred retirement plans, also known as *salary reduction plans, tax-sheltered annuities (TSAs),* and *qualified deferred compensation plans,* are named after sections of the IRS tax code. A 401(k) plan is an employer-sponsored contributory retirement savings plan in which employees divert a portion of their salary to a tax-sheltered investment account. If the employer is a tax-exempt institution, such as a public school system, college or university, hospital, or religious organization, the salary reduction plan is a 403(b) plan. Although regulations for 401(k) and 403(b) plans are different from those for IRAs, conceptually the two plans are very similar to IRAs. As is true with IRAs, federal income taxes are deferred, and state and local income taxes are often deferred, but Social Security taxes are withheld on full wages up to the established income limit.

Generally, 401(k) plans are permitted to impose two eligibility requirements. First, a minimum age of no more than twenty-one years may be required. Second, a minimum time of service of no more than one year may be required for employees. Typically, a "year of service" is a twelve-month period beginning on the first day of employment, during which time an employee completes at least 1,000 hours of service.

The limitation on the amount that can be contributed to a 401(k) plan during an employee's taxable year began in 1987, at $7,000. This amount is indexed annually for inflation, as measured by the Consumer Price Index. In 1993 the limitation was $8,994. The IRS tax code also imposes a total

Fees vary among financial institutions that offer IRAs and other tax-advantaged retirement plans. Some institutions charge a fee to open an account, while other institutions levy an annual fee to maintain an account. The fees are not universal, and it is to your advantage to shop around for the best deal. Be aware that some institutions do not levy any charges for these accounts.

limit on the combination of employee after-tax contributions, employee elective deferrals, nonelective employer contributions, and employer matching contributions that may be contributed to a 401(k) plan during a taxable year for a particular employee. In general terms, the total of these contributions may not exceed $30,000 or 25 percent of the participant's compensation, whichever is less. If an individual participates in more than one plan, it is the employee's obligation to keep track of the total limit set aside in different plans from different employers. Employees in 403(b) plans can contribute a maximum of $9,500 (or in some cases, after fifteen years of employment, up to $12,500), with the same $30,000 overall maximum. In addition to these tax-deferred contributions, some 401(k) plans allow contributions of after-tax dollars, on which the earnings remain sheltered.

In general, contributions to a 403(b) plan may not be distributed to a participant until one of the following events occurs: the participant reaches age fifty-nine and a half; separation from an employer; disability; death; plan termination; or sale of the sponsoring organization. If you change jobs, you can transfer your 401(k) or 403(b) balance to your new company if that company accepts rollovers, or you can move your balance to a rollover IRA. Some exceptions to distribution restrictions are made for early retirement and hardship conditions. As is true for IRAs, if you retire past age fifty-five but before age fifty-nine and a half, you may withdraw funds from a 401(k) or 403(b) plan without paying a penalty *if* you take the money in the form of annuity payments over your life expectancy. After five years this payout rate can be changed. Money can be withdrawn for hardships such as funeral costs, medical expenses, tuition, or a down payment on a home; however, you must prove that you have been turned down for loans and that you have exhausted all other sources of funds to pay the expenses. Furthermore, employers can impose restrictions on withdrawals, even in cases when penalties would not have to be paid. Money can be borrowed from 401(k) and 403(b) plans without paying penalties. Borrowing limits range from $10,000 to $50,000, depending upon the amount in the account, and the loan must be repaid in five years.

Keogh Plans

A Keogh plan, also called an *H.R. 10 plan,* is a qualified pension plan that was developed for self-employed individuals and their employees. Any income earned through self-employment such as writing, consulting, and child care qualifies for Keogh contributions. There are four types of Keogh plans, the first of which is a *money-purchase plan,* wherein participants may contribute up to 25 percent of *earned* income or $30,000, whichever is less. Because earned income is defined to be net earnings from self-employment less the deductible Keogh contributions, the maxi-

---

.........Although the IRS will assess a penalty on early withdrawals from an IRA, you are permitted to transfer the funds to another institution without penalty. The funds may be transferred directly from institution to institution or may be withdrawn and moved to another institution. Withdrawals must be reinvested within sixty days to avoid a penalty.

mum Keogh contribution is actually only 20 percent of net income before Keogh contributions. A disadvantage of a money-purchase Keogh plan is the requirement that you must stick with the percentage contribution you initially select. A *profit-sharing Keogh plan* removes this restriction, but the maximum contribution is 13.043 percent of net income before Keogh contributions. A *combination,* or *paired, Keogh plan* uses two accounts so that you can establish a required minimum for some years, but you are not required to contribute that much every year. Finally, there is a *defined-benefit Keogh plan* for late starters, allowing you to contribute up to 100 percent of your income up to a maximum amount ($90,000 when indexing began, in 1988). A self-employed person can have both a SEP and a Keogh plan, but aggregate annual contributions cannot exceed $30,000 or 15 percent of income. Taxes are deferred on the earnings from both contributions and the earnings in all Keogh plans until withdrawals are made.

Keogh plans are complex to establish and often have high administrative fees. There is no leeway period for making contributions after the end of a taxable year. On the positive side, money can be borrowed from a Keogh plan by paying a 5 percent, rather than a 10 percent, penalty. Unlike IRA participants, individuals receiving lump-sum distributions from Keogh plans can use five-year income averaging, and contributions can still be made after age seventy and a

---

IRAs generally provide greater flexibility than annuities. IRAs also offer lower fees that can produce a higher overall return. If your income is low enough for your IRA contributions to result in reduced taxable income, the IRA wins hands down.

---

half. Withdrawals before age fifty-nine and a half are generally penalized, but as for 401(k) and 403(b) plans, exceptions are sometimes made for early retirement and hardship conditions. If an owner-employee takes a distribution from a Keogh plan and rolls it over to an IRA, no additional contributions to the plan can be made for at least five years.

Profit-Sharing Plans and ESOPs

Employer-sponsored pension plans are usually utilized to supplement other company plans. These plans allow employees to benefit personally when the company does well. Contributions to a *profit-sharing plan* are based on the profits achieved by the employer. Contributions are large in high-profit years and small during low-profit years. Withdrawals are permitted only after the money has been in the plan for two years or the employee has participated in the plan for five years.

An *Employee Stock Ownership Plan (ESOP)*, also called a *stock bonus plan*, is a qualified retirement plan in which contributions are invested in stock of the employing corporation. Growth of the retirement nest egg depends upon the performance of the company and its stock. The stock is usually held in trust until you retire, at which time you can receive either the stock or an equivalent amount of cash.

ESOPs and profit-sharing plans tend to be risky pension plans because their values are tied to the fortunes of a single company. This risk is particularly important if an ESOP or a profit-sharing plan is the only retirement plan offered by your employer. A related risk is that your employment is tied to the same company. If things at the company go downhill, you may lose your job at the same time that the value of your retirement plan is plummeting. If possible, you should also invest in an alternative plan. Furthermore, if you are fifty-five or older and have been in an ESOP for at least ten years, you are allowed to move 25 percent of your money into other investments and should do so. Over the next five years, you can move an additional 25 percent.

Other Retirement Plans

Simplified Employee Pension Plans (SEPs) are very easy to establish (the required IRS Form 5205-SEP has only a few lines) and allow much larger annual contributions than IRAs. A regular SEP allows annual contributions of 13.043 percent of income or $30,000, whichever is less, the same as for a profit-sharing Keogh plan. Employees under age seventy and a half may contribute an additional $2,000 or 100 percent of compensation, whichever is less. Employers, known as owner-employees, who use a SEP must make contributions on behalf of every employee who is age twenty-one or older and who has worked for the employer three of the last five years. An employer can exclude employees who earn less than $300 a year or who are covered under a collective bargaining agreement. The percentage of total compensation contributed must be the *same* for each employee. Exceptions and additional restrictions apply for workers with earnings in excess of $200,000 per year. A self-employed person can contribute to a SEP as his or her own employer. Contributions for a calendar year can be made until April 15 of the following year, or even as late as August 15, if the employer receives an extension for filing his or her taxes. Lump-sum distributions from a SEP are not eligible for five-year income averaging.

Another type of plan, called a *salary reduction,* or *salary deferral, SEP,* is available for employers with twenty-five or fewer employees. At least 50 percent of eligible employees must elect to contribute to the plan, which permits maximum annual contributions of $8,994 to be sheltered from federal income taxes. Tax-deferred amounts are still subject to Social Security taxes. Employers can also contribute as long as the aggregate of both employee and employer contributions does not exceed the lesser of $30,000 or 15 percent of the employee's salary. Additional restrictions apply for "highly compensated" employees.

From an employer's point of view, a third-party-sponsored (employer-sponsored) IRA can be an alternative to a SEP. Employer-sponsored IRA plans do not have to be provided for all employees—an advantage to the employer—but there is a $2,000 limit on the annual contributions.

Retirement bonds were issued by the U.S. government prior to 1982, and they remain a part of many retirement plan portfolios. They continue to draw interest and may be redeemed before age fifty-nine and a half and rolled over tax-free.

If you are to receive a lump-sum distribution from a company retirement plan, you might consider having the funds transferred to a tax-protected IRA money market fund. This will provide you with time to determine how best to invest the money and keep you from rushing into something you will later regret.

A Comparison of Retirement Plan Alternatives

Now that you have had the opportunity to learn about various retirement savings plans, let's look at a final numerical example. Figure 35 compares the amount of money that will accumulate using three types of retirement accounts: (1) a regular savings account that is funded by after-tax income and whose earnings are taxed annually; (2) a nondeductible IRA that is also funded by after-tax income whose earnings are tax deferred; (3) a deductible IRA, 401(k) plan, Keogh plan, SEP, or other tax-deferred plan that is funded from before-tax income, with taxes on the contributions and interest earned being deferred until withdrawals are made. Although it is impossible to know what tax rates will exist at retirement (unless retirement begins next year), the benefits of tax deferral are clear. Even if the retirement tax rate stays the same, at 28 percent, a nondeductible IRA and a 401(k) plan outperform a regular account by 18 and 49 percent, respectively, after all taxes are paid! If the retirement tax rate is lower (15 percent) because of a smaller income during retirement, a nondeductible IRA and a 401(k) plan are better than a regular account by an even wider margin of 33 and 76 percent.

A 401(k) or 403(b) plan is perhaps the best investment deal available in terms of characteristics and availability and is usually preferable to an IRA for several reasons. First, the maximum amount that can be contributed annually to one of these plans is substantially higher than the maximum for an IRA. Second, 401(k) plans are available regardless of income level or participation in other retirement programs. Third, withdrawals because of financial hardship are allowed without penalty in 401(k) plans. Fourth, although

Figure 35

COMPARING THREE DIFFERENT RETIREMENT PLANS

($1,000 Annual Contributions at 8 Percent for Thirty Years)

	Regular Account	Nondeductible IRA	401(k) or Deductible IRA
Planned contributions	$30,000	$30,000	$30,000
Tax on contributions	8,400	8,400	0
Net deposit	21,600	21,600	30,000
Value at withdrawal[1]	54,741[2]	81,562	113,280
28 Percent Retirement Tax Rate			
Tax on withdrawal	$ 0	$16,789	$31,718
Net withdrawal	54,741	64,773	81,562
Gain over regular account	—	10,032	26,821
Percent Gain	—	18 percent	49 percent
15 Percent Retirement Tax Rate			
Tax on withdrawal	$ 0	$ 8,994	$16,992
Net withdrawal	54,741	72,568	96,288
Gain over regular account	—	17,827	41,547
Percentage gain	—	33 percent	76 percent

[1]A 28% tax rate is assumed during working years.

[2]A 28 percent annual tax is paid on the 8 percent interest earned, resulting in an after-tax return on the contributions of 8 percent $\times$ (1 − .28) = 5.76 percent.

money can't be borrowed from an IRA, many companies will allow employees to borrow from their own 401(k) or profit-sharing accounts. The maximum loan is the lesser of $50,000 or 50 percent of the account balance. Loans generally have to be repaid in installments over no more than five years, but sometimes loans to buy a home can run longer. Fifth, many employers (about 70 percent, according to one survey) agree to match part or all of an employee's contributions to a 401(k) plan. SEPs have most of the same advantages of 401(k) plans and larger contributions are permitted, but eligibility is more restricted. Keogh plans are also excellent, but they are restricted to self-employed persons.

Glossary

abusive tax shelter A tax shelter that improperly interprets the tax code to produce tax benefits that would be judged inappropriate by the Internal Revenue Service.

accumulation period The period of time during which annuity payments to an insurance company are paid and remain on deposit prior to the payout period.

adjusted basis The cost at which an asset is acquired, adjusted for certain other occurrences, such as commissions or fees.

adjusted gross income Gross income less certain specified deductions, such as alimony payments and contributions to a Keogh plan.

ad valorem tax A tax based on the value of an asset.

after-tax yield The yield on an asset after taxes have been subtracted.

alternative minimum tax (AMT) A federal tax based on ordinary taxable income adjusted for certain tax preferences, such as interest paid on certain types of municipal bonds. The AMT primarily affects individuals with high incomes and tax shelters.

annuity A series of payments. Various types of annuities are sold by life insurance companies.

appreciation An increase in the market value of an asset.

at-risk rule A limitation of tax write-offs to the amount of money invested.

basis For tax purposes, the amount of money invested in an asset.

beneficiary The person or organization who is designated to receive the proceeds of a life insurance policy.

capital gain The amount by which the proceeds from the sale of an asset exceed the basis.

capital gains tax A tax based on gains and losses from the sale of capital assets, such as stocks, bonds, and real estate.

cash flow The amount of cash produced by an asset over its lifetime or over the period the asset will be owned.

cash value Savings that have accumulated in a life insurance policy. Cash values accumulate because premium payments exceed the insurance company's expenses and cost of providing death benefits.

constructive dividend Payment to a stockholder that is considered to be a dividend by the Internal Revenue Service even though the paying company calls it something else.

conversion privilege The right of a policyholder to convert a group life insurance policy to an individual policy.

coupon The interest rate paid on a debt security stated as a percentage of the security's face value. A 6 percent coupon on a $1,000 bond pays $60 in annual interest to the bond-holder.

credit rating A quality grading of a borrower's ability to make interest and principal payments in a timely manner.

deduction An expenditure that can be used to reduce a tax-payer's tax liability.

deferred annuity A annuity in which payments to the annu-ity holder begin after premium payments have ended.

deferred compensation Compensation that is currently earned but not taxable until it is received at a later date.

defined-benefit pension plan A pension plan in which the employee's benefits are specified.

defined-contribution pension plan A pension plan in which the employee's contribution is specified. This type of plan does not specify benefits to be received.

depreciation Declines in the value of an asset because of physical wear and tear or economic factors. Several ac-counting methods are used to measure depreciation.

dividend On stock, the payment of earnings to a company's holders of preferred and common stock. On life insurance, a payment to policyholders who own participating policies.

double-exempt fund A mutual fund that invests in tax-free bonds issued in a particular state so that shareholders residing in that state will avoid state taxes as well as federal taxes.

Employment Retirement Security Act of 1974 (ERISA) Federal legislation that guarantees pension benefits to employees in the private sector. Restrictions apply to the guarantees.

Employee Stock Ownership Plan (ESOP) A qualified retirement plan in which employees receive shares of common stock of the company for which they work.

endowment life insurance A special type of life insurance policy that guarantees to pay the face value to (1) a beneficiary if the insured dies prior to the end of the endowment period, or (2) the insured, at the end of the endowment period.

equivalent taxable yield The taxable rate of return that provides the same after-tax yield as a given tax-free yield.

estate tax A tax on the estate of a deceased person that is calculated before any distributions are made.

estimated tax The projected tax liability on income that is not subject to withholding, such as dividends and interest.

foreign tax credit The decrease in a U.S. tax liability because of taxes paid to a foreign government during the same year.

401(k) plan A personal retirement plan in which an employee directs an employer to set aside a certain portion of the employee's salary in a tax-deferred account. Also called *salary reduction plan.*

general obligation bond (GO) The debt of a state or municipality that pledges its full financial resources and taxing power behind the payment of interest and principal.

gross income All income received by an individual except as specifically exempted by the IRS tax code.

immediate annuity A series of payments that begins immediately.

Individual Retirement Account (IRA) A custodial account in which individuals can set aside earned income in a tax-deferred retirement plan.

inheritance tax A tax levied on the heir(s) of an estate.

intangible tax A tax on the value of intangible assets, such as stocks and bonds. Intangible taxes are levied by some state and local governments but not by the federal government.

joint-survivor life annuity An annuity with payments that last as long as either of two persons remains alive.

life income option A life insurance settlement that allows the policyholder to choose a series of equal payments.

limited-payment life insurance Cash value life insurance that specifies a limited number of premium payments.

liquidation period The period during which an annuitant receives annuity payments.

liquidity The ease with which an asset can be converted to cash.

lump-sum distribution Disbursement of an individual's retirement plan benefits in a single payment.

marital deduction The deduction for tax purposes of property transferred from one spouse to another spouse.

maturity The date on which the final payment on a loan is to be made.

negative cash flow An income stream that does not cover operating and financing expenses.

nonqualified pension plan A pension plan that does not meet federal standards for certain tax advantages.

ordinary income Income that is taxed at the rates specified in the federal tax tables.

paid-up Pertaining to a life insurance policy that will remain in effect with no further premium payments.

passive activity income Income from a trade or business in which a taxpayer does not participate.

payout ratio The percentage of income after taxes that a company pays to its stockholders in dividends.

pension rollover Reinvestment of a lump-sum pension distribution into an Individual Retirement Account.

pretax income Income after adjustments and deductions, but before taxes have been deducted.

pretax yield The annual rate of return earned on an investment before taxes have been deducted from income.

profit-sharing plan A retirement plan in which a business pays a portion of its profits into its employees' tax-deferred savings accounts.

progressive tax A tax structured so that the rate of taxation increases as the amount to be taxed increases. The federal income tax is a progressive tax.

property exchange A transaction in which property is traded such that a portion or all of the capital gain is deferred.

qualifying annuity An IRS-approved annuity in which contributions may be deducted from taxable income.

realized gain A gain that has been realized from the sale of an appreciated asset. Capital gains are taxed in the period they are realized.

revenue bond A municipal bond on which payment of interest and principal is guaranteed only by revenue from the asset the bond issue finances.

salary reduction plan See *401(k) plan.*

Simplified Employee Pension Plan (SEP) A retirement plan created especially for small businesses in which contributions can be made into a tax-deferred fund by both the firm and the employee.

single-premium deferred annuity A deferred annuity purchased with one large premium payment. Income that accumulates in the annuity is deferred until withdrawals are made by the annuitant.

tax deferral A delay in the payment of taxes until sometime in the future.

tax shelter An investment that produces tax savings.

universal life insurance Life insurance that allows the insured to select varying premiums and death benefits during the contract period.

variable annuity An annuity with payments to the annuitant keyed to the performance of common stocks.

Index

A

Adjusted gross income
  allowable adjustments to, 11
  calculation of, 10–11
  exemptions of, 15
After-tax return
  calculation of, 28–32
  comparing two investments in regard to, 42
  pretax return, compared with, 28, 29
Alimony, 10, 11
Annuities
  deferred, 124–25
  immediate, 124–25
  taxation of, 126–27
  variable, 125–26
Average tax rate, 21

B

Bonds, 24
  credit ratings. *See* Municipal bonds, quality ratings of.
  interest rate changes and values of, 62–63
  original issue discounts for, 63
  tax implications of, 61–63
  zero-coupon, 52
Borrowing
  by governments, 5–7
  disadvantages of, 6–7

C

Capital gains and losses, 26, 32, 36
  basis for, 46–49
  calculation of, 46–49
  long-term vs. short-term, 48
  mutual fund shares, 65
  deferral on sale of residence, 100–101
  taxation of, 49, 51–52
  treatment of multiple gains and losses, 50–51
Cash flow, 102–3, 109, 100–13

Index

About the Author

David L. Scott is Professor of Accounting and Finance at Valdosta State University, Valdosta, Georgia. He was born in Rushville, Indiana, and received degrees from Purdue University and Florida State University before earning a Ph.D. in economics from the University of Arkansas at Fayetteville.

David has written more than two dozen books, including *Wall Street Words* (Houghton Mifflin), *How Wall Street Works* (Probus Publishers), and *The Guide to Personal Budgeting, The Guide to Investing in Common Stocks, The Guide to Investing in Bonds, The Guide to Investing in Mutual Funds, The Guide to Buying Insurance,* and *The Guide to Managing Credit* in the Globe Pequot *Money Smarts* series. He and his wife, Kay, are the authors of the two-volume *Guide to the National Park Areas* published by the Globe Pequot Press. David and Kay spend their summers traveling throughout the United States and Canada in their fourth Volkswagen Camper.

Globe Pequot Business Books

If you have found *The Guide to Tax-Saving Investing* informative, please be sure to read the following Globe Pequot business books.

Money Smarts Series

The Guide to Personal Budgeting
How to Stretch Your Dollars Through Wise Money Management, $8.95
by David L. Scott

The Guide to Investing in Common Stocks
How to Build Your Wealth by Mastering the Basic Strategies, $8.95
by David L. Scott

The Guide to Investing in Bonds
How to Build Your Wealth by Mastering the Basic Strategies, $8.95
by David L. Scott

The Guide to Investing in Mutual Funds
How to Build Your Wealth by Mastering the Basic Strategies, $8.95
by David L. Scott

The Guide to Buying Insurance
How to Secure the Coverage You Need at An Affordable Price, $9.95
by David L. Scott

The Guide to Managing Credit
How to Stretch Your Dollars Through Wise Credit Management, $8.95
by David L. Scott

For beginning investors we suggest
Learning to Invest
A Beginner's Guide to Building Personal Wealth, $9.95
by Beatson Wallace

To order any of these titles with MASTERCARD or VISA, call toll-free (800) 243–0495. Free shipping on three or more books ordered; $3.00 shipping charge per book on one or two books ordered. Connecticut residents add sales tax. Please request a complimentary catalogue of other quality Globe Pequot titles, which include books on travel, outdoor recreation, nature, gardening, cooking, nature, and more.

Prices and availability subject to change.